Learn the Secrets o
Numerology, Tarot, AND
AND PREDICT YOUR FUTURE

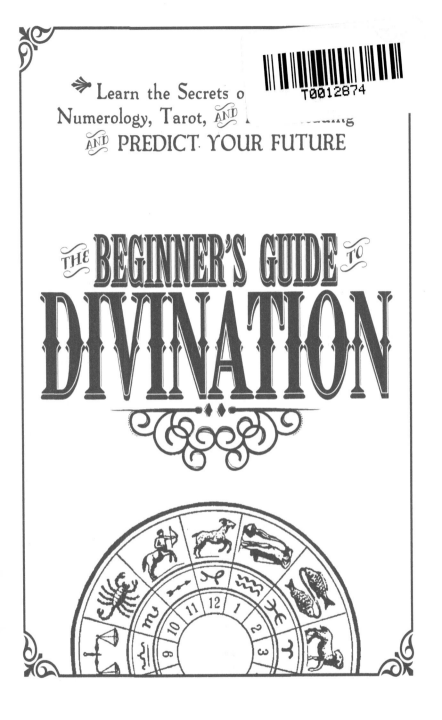

THE BEGINNER'S GUIDE TO
DIVINATION

ADAMS MEDIA
NEW YORK LONDON TORONTO SYDNEY NEW DELHI

Adams Media
An Imprint of Simon & Schuster, Inc.
100 Technology Center Drive
Stoughton, MA 02072

For information about special discounts for bulk purchases, please contact Simon & Schuster Special Sales at 1-866-506-1949 or business@simonandschuster.com.

The Simon & Schuster Speakers Bureau can bring authors to your live event. For more information or to book an event contact the Simon & Schuster Speakers Bureau at 1-866-248-3049 or visit our website at www.simonspeakers.com.

Illustrations from the Rider-Waite Tarot Deck® reproduced by permission of U.S. Games Systems, Inc., Stamford, CT 06902 U.S.A. Copyright © 1971 by U.S. Games Systems, Inc. Further reproduction prohibited. The Universal Waite Tarot Deck® is a registered trademark of U.S. Games Systems, Inc.

Manufactured in the United States of America

5 2021

Library of Congress Cataloging-in-Publication Data has been applied for.

ISBN 978-1-4405-9482-3
ISBN 978-1-4405-9483-0 (ebook)

This publication is designed to provide accurate and authoritative information with regard to the subject matter covered. It is sold with the understanding that the publisher is not engaged in rendering legal, accounting, or other professional advice. If legal advice or other expert assistance is required, the services of a competent professional person should be sought.
—From a *Declaration of Principles* jointly adopted by a Committee of the American Bar Association and a Committee of Publishers and Associations

Many of the designations used by manufacturers and sellers to distinguish their products are claimed as trademarks. Where those designations appear in this book and Simon & Schuster, Inc., was aware of a trademark claim, the designations have been printed with initial capital letters.

Contains material adapted from *The Everything® Astrology Book, 2nd Edition* by Jenni Kosarin, copyright © 2006, 1999 by Simon & Schuster, Inc., ISBN 13: 978-1-59337-373-3; *The Everything® Tarot Book, 2nd Edition* by Skye Alexander, copyright © 2006 by Simon & Schuster, Inc., ISBN 13: 978-1-59337-656-7; *The Everything® Numerology Book* by Ellae Elinwood, copyright © 2003 by Simon & Schuster, Inc., ISBN 13: 978-1-58062-700-9; *The Everything® Palmistry Book* by Katina Z. Jones, copyright © 2003 by Simon & Schuster, Inc., ISBN 13: 978-1-58062-876-1.

CONTENTS

INTRODUCTION

Do you want to see the future of your relationships in the stars? Use the power of numbers to influence your career? Divine your future health just by looking at the palm of your hand?

The Beginner's Guide to Divination gives you all this information! You'll learn everything you need to know about astrology, tarot, numerology, and palmistry and how you can use these ancient arts to predict your destiny and influence your future.

In Part 1 you'll find information on the importance of Sun signs, Moons signs, and rising signs; how to read and evaluate an astrological birth chart; and how to use this information to divine the future of your love life and your relationships with your current or future partners, no matter their signs. Part 2 gives you a background on the major and minor cards (arcana) found in the tarot deck; how to interpret the different combinations of cards; and how those cards can be read to give you perspective on what's to come. Part 3 will tell you everything you need to now about the art of numerology, including the importance of numbers as spiritual communicators, and how you can use the power of numbers to be lucky in love, enjoy successful relationships, and prosper in the career of your choice. And, finally, Part 4 will teach you how to interpret the lines, mounts, and appearance of your hands and fingers to divine your future.

So, whether you've heard of these mystical techniques and just want to learn their secrets or are interested in expanding your fortune-telling abilities, it's time to use the light of these ancient arts to illuminate the path of your future.

PART I
ASTROLOGY

Astrology is based on the belief that the movement of the stars and other celestial bodies affects our lives here on Earth. This part will catch you up on the basics of astrology, from philosophy to signs and symbols. One common misinterpretation of astrology is that it determines our fate. The truth, however, is that astrology describes our potential; it is our choice to live up to that potential or to deny it. Astrology is organic rather than mechanistic; its meaning grows and deepens as we learn its symbols and begin to understand its language. Astrology can't really predict what happens to us in day-to-day life because it deals with trends—not minute-to-minute occurrences.

So can astrology predict the future? Yes and no. By studying your chart and its relation to the stars and planets, you'll get a glimpse of periods of time. For example, you'll get a sense of a good time to ask for a raise, a great time for new love, the right time to sign or not sign a contract, or the time to move or to stay put. However, *you* are the one who needs to take advantage of the good timing.

Eventually, as you learn from this part and begin trusting your intuition, you'll come to realize that we really are masters of our own destiny. We choose it all; before birth our souls select the circumstances into which we are born. They pick the optimal astrological conditions that will allow us the opportunity to develop and evolve spiritually. These conditions are outward expressions of internal needs and help create the reality we experience. Within these patterns, our free will reigns supreme.

CHAPTER I

SUN SIGNS

Your Sun sign is the pattern of your overall personality and represents your ego. The sign in which your Sun falls influences the goals you choose and how you accomplish those goals. The twelve Sun signs are divided roughly by months, but because those divisions don't follow the months exactly, you may have been born on the cusp between two signs. If you were, then read the interpretations for both signs to divine your future. For instance, if you were born on April 19, the cutoff date for Aries, also read the interpretation for Taurus, because some of those attributes probably apply to you.

Aries

The Ram (March 21–April 19)
Element: Fire
Quality: Cardinal
Keyword: Leadership, the pioneer spirit
Planetary Ruler: Mars
Rules: Head and face; natural ruler of first house

Aries are bold, courageous, and resourceful. They always seem to know what they believe, what they want from life, and where they're going. Aries people are dynamic and aggressive (sometimes, to a fault) in pursuing their goals—whatever they might be. They're also survivors.

The challenge with this sign is lack of persistence: Aries people sometimes lose interest if they don't see rapid results. But this tendency is compensated for by their ambition and drive to succeed. They can be argumentative, lack tact, and have bad tempers. On the other hand, their anger rarely lasts long, and they can be warm and loving with those they care about.

Taurus
The Bull (April 20–May 20)
Element: Earth
Quality: Fixed
Keywords: Endurance, perseverance, stubbornness
Planetary Ruler: Venus
Rules: Neck, throat, cervical vertebrae;
natural ruler of second house

While Aries is out pioneering and discovering new lands, Taurus is settling and cultivating the land and using his resources for practical purposes. His stubbornness and determination keep him around for the long haul on any project or endeavor.

Taureans are the most stubborn sign in the zodiac. They are also incredibly patient, singular in their pursuit of goals, and determined to attain what they want. Although they lack versatility because of the fixed nature of the sign, they compensate for it by enduring whatever they have to in order to get what they want. Long after other contestants have fallen out of the race, Taurus individuals are still in the running. As a result, they often succeed where others fail.

Most Taureans enjoy being surrounded by nice things. They like fine art and music, and many have considerable musical ability. They also have a talent for working with their hands—gardening, woodworking, and sculpting.

It takes a lot to anger a Taurus person, but once you do, clear out. The "bull's rush" can be fierce. But thanks to Venus ruling this sign, Taurus people are usually sensual and romantic. They are also physically oriented individuals who take pride in their bodies.

Gemini
The Twins (May 21–June 21)
Element: Air
Quality: Mutable
Keyword: Versatility
Planetary Ruler: Mercury
Rules: Hands, arms, lungs, nervous system;
natural ruler of the third house

After Aries and Taurus have discovered and cultivated new land, Gemini ventures out to see what else is there and seizes upon new ideas that will expand their communities. Their innate curiosity keeps these people on the move.

Geminis, because they're ruled by Mercury, tend to use the rational, intellectual mind to explore and understand their personal worlds. They need to answer the single burning question in their minds: Why? This applies to most facets of their lives, from the personal to the impersonal. This need to know may send them off to foreign countries, particularly if the Sun is in the ninth house, where their need to explore other cultures and traditions ranks high.

Geminis are changeable and often moody! Their symbol, the twins, means they are often at odds with themselves—the mind demanding one thing, the heart demanding the opposite. To someone else, this internal conflict often manifests as two very different people. As a Gemini's significant other, you might reach a point where you wonder which twin you're with!

These individuals are fascinated by relationships and connections among people, places, and objects. Their rational analysis of everything, from ideas to relationships, drives them as crazy as it drives everyone else around them. When this quality leads them into an exploration of psychic and spiritual realms, it grounds them. In romance, the heart of a Gemini is won by seduction of the mind.

Cancer
The Crab (June 22–July 22)
Element: Water
Quality: Cardinal
Keyword: Nurturing, emotional drive
Planetary Ruler: Moon
Rules: Breasts, stomach, digestive system;
natural ruler of the fourth house

Once Aries, Taurus, and Gemini have discovered, settled, and expanded their new land, Cancer comes along and tames it— civilizes it. These people need roots, a place or even a state of mind that they can call their own. They need a safe harbor, a refuge in which to retreat for solitude.

Imagination, sensitivity, and the nurturing instinct characterize this sign. Cancerians are generally gentle and kind people, unless they're hurt. Then they can become vindictive and sharp-spoken. They forgive easily, but rarely forget. Cancerians tend to be affectionate, passionate, and even possessive at times. As parents, they may be overprotective. As spouses or significant others, they may smother their mates with love and good intentions.

Emotionally, Cancerians act and react in the same way the crab moves—sideways. They avoid confrontations and usually aren't comfortable in discussing what they feel. They're reluctant to reveal who they are and sometimes hide behind their protective urges, preferring to tend to the needs of others rather than to their own needs.

Cancers are intuitive and can sometimes be psychic. Experience flows through them emotionally. They're often moody and always changeable; their interests and social circles shift constantly. Once a Cancer trusts you, however, he lets you in on his most private world.

Leo
The Lion (July 23–August 22)
Element: Fire
Quality: Fixed
Keywords: Action, power
Planetary Ruler: Sun
Rules: Heart, back, and spinal cord;
natural ruler of the fifth house

Leos roar. They love being the center of attention and often surround themselves with admirers. To remain in the proud kingdom of a Leo, her admirers have to think like she thinks, believe what she believes, and hate and love whom she hates and loves. To a Leo, this is loyalty. In return, Leo offers generosity, warmth, and compassion.

Don't ever argue to change the opinions and beliefs of a Leo! You won't succeed, and the Leo will just get annoyed with you! As a fixed sign, Leos stand firm in their belief systems. They have found what works for them and don't understand why their beliefs might not work for someone else. In general, though, they are optimistic, honorable, loyal, and ambitious.

Leos have an innate dramatic sense, and life is definitely their stage. Their flamboyance and personal magnetism extend to every facet of their lives. They seek to succeed and make an impact in every situation. It is no surprise that the theater and allied arts fall under the rule of Leo.

Virgo

The Virgin (August 23–September 22)
Element: Earth
Quality: Mutable
Keywords: Order, detailed, dedication
Planetary Ruler: Mercury
Rules: Intestines, abdomen, female reproductive system;
natural ruler of the sixth house

The popular image of a Virgo is a picky, critical, and compulsively tidy person. This is misleading. If one or all of these traits manifest obviously, then the natal chart reveals other aspects that enhance this characteristic.

Virgos are like Geminis in terms of mental quickness and agility. Due to their attention to detail, they tend to delve more deeply into subjects they study. Even though they are career-oriented people, they seem to be more interested in doing their jobs efficiently and well. They're happiest when engaged in something that benefits society at large. In other words, duty is important to Virgos.

Virgos tend to be attracted to people who are intellectually stimulating or eccentric in some way. Their standards are high when it comes to romantic relationships, and unless the mental connection exists, the relationship won't last long. In their twenties, many Virgos fall for those who aren't quite good enough for them. They find critical partners or those who don't appreciate them fully—an unhealthy match.

Since Virgos, like Geminis, are Mercury-ruled, they need outlets for all their nervous energy. Running, martial arts, or workouts at the gym are recommended. Writing, pets, reading, and extra education can also serve this purpose.

Libra
The Scales (September 23–October 22)
Element: Air
Quality: Cardinal
Keyword: Balance
Planetary Ruler: Venus
Rules: Lower back and the diaphragm;
natural ruler of the seventh house

Librans seem to come in three distinct types: those who are decisive, those who aren't, and those who seek harmony for its own sake. The typical Libra seeks to mediate and balance. Librans have an inherent need to act democratically, diplomatically, and fairly—always.

In love, Libras are natural romantics and flourish in enduring partnerships. They are fair-minded people, but avoid anything that is grim, crude, vulgar, or garish. Adversely afflicted, they have trouble making decisions and may lose themselves in sensual pleasures. In highly evolved Librans, the human mind finds the perfect blend between balance and discretion.

They love beauty in all its guises—art, literature, classical music, opera, mathematics, and the human body. They usually are team players who enjoy debate but not argument. They're excellent strategists and masters at the power of suggestion. Even though Librans are courteous, amiable people, one should never presume that they're pushovers. They use diplomacy and intelligence to get what they want.

Scorpio
The Scorpion (October 23–November 21)
Element: Water
Quality: Fixed
Keywords: Regeneration, transformation
Planetary Ruler: Mars and Pluto
Rules: Sexual organs, rectum, and reproductive system;
natural ruler of the eighth house

Note the sharp point at the tip of the glyph that represents this sign. Symbolically, it's the scorpion's stinger, which characterizes the biting sarcasm often associated with Scorpios. These people are intense, passionate, and strong-willed. They often impose their will on others. In less aware people, this can manifest as cruelty, sadism, and enmity; in the more evolved Scorpio, this characteristic transforms lives for the better. Like Aries, Scorpios aren't afraid of anything. But they have an endurance that Aries lacks that enables them to plow ahead and overcome whatever opposition they encounter.

Scorpios don't know the meaning of indifference. They either approve or disapprove, agree or disagree. You're either a friend or an enemy: there are no shades of gray. Once you've gained a Scorpio's trust, you've won his loyalty forever—unless you hurt him or someone he loves. Then they can become vindictive enemies.

Scorpios possess an innate curiosity and suspicion of easy answers that compels them to probe deeply into whatever interests them. They dig out concealed facts and seek the meaning behind facades. Most Scorpios are exceptionally intuitive, even if they don't consciously acknowledge it. The more highly evolved people in this sign are often very psychic, with rich inner lives and passionate involvement in metaphysics.

Scorpios are industrious and relentless workers. They excel at anything associated with the eighth house—trusts/inheritances, psychological counseling, and the occult. Sometimes they're more passionate with their work than they are with the important people in their lives.

Sagittarius
The Archer (November 22–December 21)
Element: Fire
Quality: Mutable
Keywords: Idealism, freedom
Planetary Ruler: Jupiter
Rules: Hips, thighs, liver, and hepatic system;
natural ruler of the ninth house

These people seek the truth, express it as they see it—and don't care if anyone else agrees with them. They see the large picture of any issue and can't be bothered with the mundane details. They are always outspoken and can't understand why other people aren't as candid. After all, what is there to hide?

This is a mentally oriented sign where logic reigns supreme. But the mentality differs from Gemini, the polar opposite of Sagittarius, in several important ways. A Gemini is concerned with the here and now: he needs to know how and why things and relationships work in his life. A Sagittarian, however, focuses on the future and on the larger family of humanity. Quite often, this larger family includes animals—large, small, wild, or domestic—and the belief that all deserve the right to live free.

Despite Sagittarians' propensity for logic, they are often quite prescient, with an uncanny ability to glimpse the future. Even when they have this ability, however, they often think they need an external tool to trigger it such as tarot cards, an astrology chart, or runes. Many Sagittarians reject the idea of astrology, as well—they rely solely on practicality and inherent intuition.

They love their freedom and chafe at any restrictions. Their versatility and natural optimism win them many friends, but only a few ever really know the heart of the Sagittarian.

Capricorn

The Goat (December 22–January 19)
Element: Earth
Quality: Cardinal
Keywords: Materialism, self-discipline
Planetary Ruler: Saturn
Rules: Knees, skin, and bones; natural ruler of the tenth house

Capricorns are serious-minded people who often seem aloof and tightly in control of their emotions and their personal domain. Even as youngsters, there's a mature air about them, as if they were born with a profound core that few outsiders ever see.

This sign's nickname, the goat, represents Capricorn's slow, steady rise through the world. They're easily impressed by outward signs of success, but are interested less in money than in the power that money represents. Like Scorpio, they feel the need to rule whatever kingdom they occupy whether this is their home, workplace, or business. Like Scorpios, they prize power and mastery over others, but they tend to be subtler about it.

Capricorns are true workers—industrious, efficient, and disciplined. They deplore inertia in other people. Their innate common sense gives them the ability to plan ahead and to work out practical ways of approaching goals. More often than not, they succeed at whatever they set out to do.

In a crowd, Capricorns aren't particularly easy to spot. They aren't physically distinctive the way Scorpios are, and they aren't the life of the party like Sagittarians. But they possess a quiet dignity that's unmistakable.

Aquarius
Water Bearer (January 20–February 18)
Element: Air
Quality: Fixed
Planetary Ruler: Uranus
Keywords: Altruism, individuality, freedom
Rules: Ankles, shins, and circulatory system;
natural ruler of the eleventh house

Aquarians are original thinkers, often eccentric, who prize individuality and freedom above all else. The tribal mentality goes against their grain. They chafe at the restrictions placed upon them by society and seek to follow their own paths.

Aquarius is the sign of true genius because these people generally have the ability to think in unique ways. Once they make up their minds about something, nothing can convince them to change what they believe. This stubbornness is a double-edged sword; it can sustain them or destroy them. When the stubbornness manifests in small rebellions against the strictures of society, energy is wasted that could be put to better use.

Even though compassion is a hallmark of this Sun sign, Aquarians usually don't become emotionally involved with the causes they promote. Their compassion, while genuine, rises from the intellect rather than the heart. The Uranian influence confers a fascination with a broad spectrum of intellectual interests.

Pisces
The Fish (February 19–March 20)
Element: Water
Quality: Mutable
Keywords: Compassion, mysticism
Planetary Ruler: Neptune
Rules: Externally, the feet and toes; internally, Pisces rules the
lymphatic system; natural ruler of the twelfth house

Pisces need to explore their world through their emotions. They feel things so deeply that quite often they become a kind of psychic sponge, absorbing the emotions of people around them. Because of this, they should choose their friends and associates carefully.

People born under this sign usually have wonderful imaginations and great creative resources. They gravitate toward the arts, in general, and to theater and film, in particular. In the business world, they make powerful administrators and managers because they are so attuned to the thoughts of the people around them.

Pisces people need time alone so that they can detach from the emotions of people around them and center themselves. They are very impressionable. Without periodic solitude, it becomes increasingly difficult for them to sort out what they feel from what other people feel. They also tend to be moody because they feel the very height of joy and the utter depths of despair. Love and romance are essential for most Piscean individuals. These fulfill them emotionally, and Pisces generally flourish within stable relationships.

CHAPTER 2

UNDERSTANDING THE PLANETS

Intuition can bring any birth chart interpretation into clarity. It is the essential connection that links the pieces into a coherent whole—a living story. Without intuition, you're just reading symbols. Knowledge and understanding of the planets will give you a broad base to start from and a context in which to consider those symbols. For instance, one thing you should know is that planets are the expression of energy. They are classified as benefic or malefic: good or bad. In this chapter, you'll find out more about this and other characteristics of the planets.

In addition, the sign a planet occupies describes how that particular energy permeates your personality and influences your life. If you have eight out of nine planets (and Pluto) in Fire signs, then you probably have abundant energy and a fierce temper, and tend to initiate action. If you have mostly Air planets, your approach to life comes from a mental standpoint— rationalizing and thinking before acting. For each planet, you'll find information about the importance of planets in the signs.

Inner and Outer Planets

Planets orbit the Sun at different speeds. The closer a planet is to the Sun, the faster it travels through its orbit. The Moon, for instance, travels through the zodiac in about twenty-eight days and spends two to three days in each sign. Mercury orbits the Sun in eighty-eight days. Pluto, which lies the farthest from the Sun, completes its orbit in 248 years. The faster moving planets—Moon, Mercury, Venus, Mars—are known as inner planets. Jupiter, Uranus, Neptune, and Pluto are known as outer planets.

The luminaries—Sun and Moon—have transpersonal qualities. The Sun represents not only our ego, but fundamental cosmic energy. The Moon, which concerns our most intimate emotions and urges, links us to what astrologer Robert Hand calls, "One's Ultimate Source."

Note: Pluto was demoted from planetary status in 2006 but that decision is subject to change and is still being debated. Meanwhile, astrologers continue to use its influence.

Planetary Motion

Planetary motion is either direct (D), retrograde (R), or stationary (S). In reality, all planetary motion is direct but relative motion isn't. The Sun and the Moon can never turn retrograde, but all the other planets do. A retrograde planet is one that appears to move backward in the zodiac, but this backward motion is actually an optical illusion. Imagine being in a train as another train speeds past you. You feel as if you're moving backward, when in actuality, you're only moving more slowly than the other train. Retrograde motion doesn't change the fundamental essence of a planet; it merely means that the expression of its energy is altered somewhat.

During a retrograde, the nature of that planet is forced inward, where it creates tension and stress. The outlet for this tension is usually worked out in relationships with others.

Planets in direct motion have more influence than retrograde planets. Stationary planets, those that are about to turn direct or retrograde, have greater influence in a chart than either retrograde or direct-moving planets. This is due to the concentrated energy of the planet.

Strengths and Weaknesses of the Planets

The strength or weakness of a planet depends on its sign, placement in the houses, aspects, and motion. A planet that occupies a sign it rules is *dignified*—Mercury in Gemini, for instance, or Venus in Libra.

When a planet is *exalted* its drive and essential qualities are expressed more harmoniously. An example would be the Sun in Aries or the Moon in Taurus. Exalted planets are assigned specific degrees and are said to function smoothly within those degrees.

A planet is in the sign of *detriment* when it occupies the sign opposite that of its dignity. An example is Mercury in Sagittarius. Mercury is in detriment here because it rules Gemini, and Sagittarius is Gemini's polar opposite. In a detriment, the energy of the planet is considered to be at a disadvantage. When a planet lies in the sign opposite that of its exaltation, it's said to be *in fall*. A Moon in Scorpio is in fall because the Moon is exalted in Taurus. Its energy is watered down.

Mutual reception occurs when two planets are placed in each other's sign of dignity. The Sun and the Moon, for instance, are in mutual reception if the Sun is in Cancer or Taurus, and the Moon is in Leo or Aries. This happens because the Sun rules Leo and is exalted in Aries, and the Moon rules Cancer and is exalted in Taurus. When a planet is placed in its natural house of the horoscope (Mercury in the third house, for instance), it's *accidentally dignified* and strengthened.

Sun and Moon: Ego and Emotions

The Sun is the very essence and energy of life—the manifestation of will, power, and desire. It represents the ego, individuality, the yang principle and is the thrust that allows us to meet challenges and expand our lives. The Sun represents a person's creative abilities and the general state of his or her physical health.

The Sun embraces the fatherhood principle and in a chart, symbolizes a person's natural father and a woman's husband. As natural ruler of the fifth house, it rules children in general and the firstborn in particular. Leo is ruled by the Sun—fire.

The Sun spends about a month in each sign, with a mean daily motion of 59'8". It rules occupations of power and authority—royalty and religious and spiritual rulers. Its natural house is the fifth, and it governs the sign of Leo. It rules the heart, back, spine, and spinal cord.

The Moon is your emotions—the inner you. It's intuition, the mother, the yin principle. Coupled with the Sun and the ascendant, the Moon is one of the vital parts of a chart. It describes our emotional reactions to situations, how emotions flow through us, motivating and compelling us—or limiting us and holding us back.

The Moon symbolizes a person's mother and the relationship between mother and child. In a man's chart, the Moon represents his wife; in a woman's chart, it describes pregnancies, childbirth, and intuition. Symbolically, the Moon represents our capacity to become part of the whole rather than attempting to master the parts. It asks that we become whatever it is that we seek.

As Earth's satellite, the Moon moves more swiftly than any of the planets, completing a circuit of the zodiac in less than twenty-eight days. It rules activities and professions dealing with children and those that concern the sea. Its natural house is the fourth and it governs the sign of Cancer. The stomach, breasts, mammary glands, womb, conception, and the body fluids in general are ruled by the Moon.

The Moon in the Signs

Aries Moon. Your emotions are all fire. You're passionate, impulsive, and headstrong. Your relationships, especially when you're younger, can be impulsive. Your own actions ground you. You take pride in your ability to make decisions and to get things moving.

Taurus Moon (exalted). You don't like to argue. You need time alone and thrive in your private spaces, whatever they might be. You enjoy your creature comforts and being surrounded by belongings that hold personal meaning. Your emotional well-being depends on the harmony of your emotional attachments.

Gemini Moon. You thrive on change and variety. Your emotions fluctuate and sometimes you think too much, analyzing what you feel and why. Your capacity for adaptability, however, sees you through the many changes you experience.

Cancer Moon (dignified). You have strong family ties and feel a need to nurture or nourish others. At times, you're very psychic; other times you're merely moody. When you're hurt, you tend to withdraw and brood. You don't like emotional confrontations and seek to sidestep them.

Leo Moon. Your emotions are often dramatic. You feel cheerful and optimistic about life in general. You enjoy the limelight and being recognized for what you do and who you are. You take deep pride in your children and family.

Virgo Moon. You tend to be somewhat reticent about what you feel. You're interested in health and hygiene and how these issues relate to you and the people you care for. You feel happy when you're of service to others and take pride in your meticulous attention to details. You can be overly critical of your personal relationships and of yourself.

Libra Moon. Discord makes you feel anxious. You thrive on harmony in your personal environment and need compatible relationships for your emotional well-being. You go out of your way to avoid confrontations. Music, art, ballet, and literature lift your spirits.

Scorpio Moon (in fall). Your emotions and passions run deep. You feel a profound loyalty to your family and the people you love. You possess great strength and are able to draw on it during times of crisis. Your dreams, premonitions, and many of your experiences border on the mystical. You rarely forget it when someone has slighted you.

Sagittarius Moon. You need emotional freedom and independence. You need your own space so you can explore everything that fascinates you—foreign cultures, inner worlds, or the distant future. None of this means that you love your significant other any less; you simply need your freedom. You enjoy animals.

Capricorn Moon (detriment). You need structure of some sort to feel emotionally secure. This need can show up in any area of your life; it depends on what issues are important to you at a given time. You aren't as emotionally aloof as some people think; you just don't wear your heart on your sleeve.

Aquarius Moon. Your compassion extends to humanity— the beggar on Seventh Avenue, the children dying in Africa, or the AIDS patients whose families have turned against them. You bleed for them. Your home life is important to you, but it's definitely not traditional. You don't recognize boundaries or limitations of any sort.

Pisces Moon. When your emotions flow through you with the ease of water, you feel and sense what is invisible to others. Sometimes, you're a psychic sponge; you soak up emotions from others and may even manifest those emotions. Your compassion sometimes makes you gullible and impractical. Your artistic sensibilities are strong.

Mercury: Your Intellect

Mental quickness. Verbal acuity. Communication. Your mental picture of the world. Mercury is the messenger; it speaks in terms of logic and reasoning. The left brain is its vehicle. Mercury represents how we think and how we communicate those thoughts. Mercury also is concerned with travel of the routine variety—work commutes, trips across town, weekend excursions, or a visit with siblings and neighbors—rather than long-distance travel.

Mercury orbits the Sun in about eighty-eight days. It goes retrograde every few months, and, during that time, communications and travel plans go haywire. Your computer may go down, lightning may blow out your electricity, or you may spend hours in an airport waiting for a flight that is ultimately canceled. Again, it's best not to sign contracts when Mercury is retrograde.

Mercury rules any profession dealing with writing, teaching, speaking, books, and publications. Mercury is the natural ruler of the third and sixth houses and governs Gemini and Virgo. It rules arms, hands, shoulders, lungs, the solar plexus, abdomen, intestines, the thymus gland, and the nervous and respiratory systems.

Mercury in the Signs

Mercury in Aries. You have a quick, decisive mind that makes snap judgments. You're often argumentative but intuitive about the dynamics of relationships.

Mercury in Taurus. Yours is a practical, determined mind with strong likes and dislikes. You have intuition about the practical aspects of relationships and love beautiful, flowing language. You can be quite stubborn.

Mercury in Gemini (dignified). Marked by a quick, inventive mind, you're up to date on current events and have shrewd powers of observation. You have an adaptable, versatile intellect, ease with language, and intuition about the structure of relationships. You also enjoy travel.

Mercury in Cancer. Your sensitive, imaginative mind also has excellent powers of retention. However, your opinions change quickly. You're interested in psychic matters and may have psychic abilities as well. You're intuitive about the inner connections in relationships.

Mercury in Leo (in fall). Great willpower and lofty ideals characterize you. Your intellect can be self-centered, but intuitive. Your mental aspirations may revolve around children, pets, drama, and sports. Your intellectual efforts often carry your personal unique style.

Mercury in Virgo. You have facility with language and as a linguist. Mentally, you display great attention to detail, which can collapse into criticism and nitpicky tendencies. There's a deep interest in mystery, the occult, and magic, and you have excellent intellect overall.

Mercury in Libra. Yours is a refined intellect, capable of broad scope. You are excellent at balancing issues and intuitive about the innate balance in relationships. This is good placement for any artistic pursuit, particularly music.

Mercury in Scorpio. You have a suspicious but deeply intuitive intellect capable of probing beneath the obvious. You also have a mental need to perceive the hidden order of things, to pierce that order, and pull out the truth. You can be sarcastic and wry in communication.

Mercury in Sagittarius (detriment). You're idealistic and intellectually versatile. Mental and intellectual development comes through philosophy, religion, law, publishing, and travel. Your personal opinions sometimes are inflated and become principles rather than just personal opinions.

Mercury in Capricorn. You're characterized by mental discipline and organizational ability. Your intellect is sometimes structured in a way that inhibits imagination. You experience much serious and thoughtful contemplation.

Mercury in Aquarius (exalted). Your intellect is detached from emotion and endlessly inventive. Your mental interests tend to be progressive, unusual, and often eccentric. You exhibit interest in the occult and science.

Mercury in Pisces (detriment). Your psychic impressions are often so pronounced that reasoning ability is clouded. Great imagination and creativity are indicated and much information is culled through intuitive means.

Venus: Your Love Life

Romance. Beauty. Artistic instinct. Sociability. Venus governs our ability to attract compatible people, to create close personal relationships, and to form business partnerships. It expresses how we relate to other people one-on-one and how we express ourselves in marriage and in romantic relationships.

Venus is also associated with the arts and the aesthetic sense, and it has enormous influence on our tastes in art, music, and literature. The sign and placement of Venus, as well as its aspects, determine our refinement—or lack of it. This planet also has some bearing on material resources, earning capacity, and spending habits. A strong Venus enhances these things; a poorly placed or badly aspected Venus generates laziness, self-indulgence, extravagance, and discord in partnerships.

Venus orbits the Sun in 255 days. It spends about four weeks in a sign when moving directly and is retrograde for about six weeks. It rules all professions having to do with the arts and music. Its natural houses are the second and the seventh, and it governs Taurus and Libra. It rules the neck, throat, thyroid gland, kidneys, ovaries, veins, and circulation of the venous blood. It shares rulership with the Moon over the female sex organs.

Venus in the Signs
Venus in Aries (detriment). You exhibit aggressive social interaction and passion in romantic relationships. You form impetuous, impulsive ties and are self-centered in love. You show

good initiative in making money, but it usually goes out as fast as it comes in. For you, marriage may happen early or in haste.

Venus in Taurus (dignified). Heightened artistic expression. You attract money and material resources easily. You form deeply emotional love attachments. You have strong financial drive. Marriage is sometimes delayed when Venus is in Taurus.

Venus in Gemini. You're flirtatious and exude great charm and wit. You're a good conversationalist, you're popular, and you enjoy reading and travel. You also have a tendency for short-lived relationships, which can occur simultaneously. You're a spendthrift who earns money from a variety of sources. You will have several occupations and, possibly, several marriages as well.

Venus in Cancer. Home and marriage are important and offer you a sense of security. Family ties are strong. You spend money on home and family, but also squirrel it away in savings. You benefit through houses, land, and wide, open spaces. Being near water gives you a sense of tranquility.

Venus in Leo. You're ardent in relationships and have a gregarious nature. You may have a pronounced talent in one of the arts. You like to entertain and gamble and have a strong attraction to the opposite sex. You gain through investments and speculation.

Venus in Virgo (in fall). Secret romances, disappointment through love, and possibly more than one marriage may befall you. You're too analytical and criticize romantic relationships and emotions. You're a perfectionist about artistic self-expression.

Venus in Libra (dignified). You have a kind, sympathetic nature and love the arts, music, and drama. You have a happy marriage with talented children. You earn money through areas that Venus rules and seek harmony in all your relationships.

Venus in Scorpio (detriment). You have a passionate nature and dominant sex drive. For you, marriage can be delayed and relationships are often stormy. Your friends may have mystical and occult talents. You gain financially through inheritances, taxes, insurance, and the occult.

Venus in Sagittarius. You have generous nature and ardent emotions in love. If your relationships threaten your personal freedom, however, your emotions cool rapidly. Love of arts, travel, and animals, with a particular fondness for horses, characterizes you. There can be more than one marriage.

Venus in Capricorn. You exercise restraint in emotions and experience some disappointment in love and romance. Marriage is usually for practical reasons and may be to someone older and more established financially. The partner may be cold and indifferent. Your emphasis is on acquiring financial and material assets.

Venus in Aquarius. You have friends from all walks of life and strange, unexpected experiences in romance and friendships. You have a need for intellectual stimulation in romantic partnerships and exhibit erratic financial habits. You gain through friends, partnerships, and speculations.

Venus in Pisces (exalted). You have a charitable, compassionate nature. More than one marriage is likely for you. Romantic love and emotional attachments are necessary to your well-being. You exhibit great sensitivity to others and psychic abilities are likely.

Mars: Your Energy

Dynamic expression. Aggression. Individualism. Sexual drive. Action. Mars dictates our survival energy and the shape that energy assumes as we define ourselves in terms of the larger world. It represents the individualization process, particularly in a romantic relationship. A weak Mars placement in a woman's chart may make her too passive and submissive in a love relationship, especially if her significant other has a strongly placed Mars.

Mars rules athletes and competitions. The true Mars individual seeks to take himself to the limit—and then surpass that limit.

He refuses to compromise his integrity by following another's agenda. He doesn't compare himself to other people and doesn't want to dominate or be dominated. He simply wants to be free to follow his own path, whatever it is.

Mars orbits the Sun in 687 days. It spends six to eight weeks in a sign. When retrograde, it sits in a sign for two and half months. As the god of war, Mars governs the military, rules Aries, and is co-ruler of Scorpio. Its natural houses are the first and the eighth. It rules the head, general musculature of the body, the sex organs in general—the male sex organs in particular—the anus, red corpuscles, and hemoglobin.

Mars in the Signs

Mars in Aries (dignified). You go after what you want. Your strong sex drive sometimes manifests selfishly, with little regard for the partner. Initiative and drive are highly developed, but due to haste and impulsiveness, there can be a tendency not to finish what you've started.

Mars in Taurus (detriment). You're not easily thwarted or discouraged by obstacles. Your sheer determination and strength of will are well developed, but may not be used to the fullest. You prefer purposeful, practical action to achieve what you want. Your sexual nature is sensual, but can be somewhat passive. You find pleasure through your profession.

Mars in Gemini. Energy is expressed mentally, through a keen intellect and versatile mind. You tend to take on too many projects that scatter your energy. Your mental restlessness needs a creative outlet or otherwise you become argumentative. You enjoy travel, science, and law. This is good placement for writing.

Mars in Cancer (in fall). You take everything personally and find it difficult to be objective about issues that are important to you. Your sex drive is overshadowed by deep emotional needs.

Mars in Leo. Passion rules the expression of your energy. You possess good leadership ability, a fearless nature, and a determined will. You need to be appreciated for who you are and as a lover. Mechanical or musical skill may be indicated.

Mars in Virgo. You express your energy through efficient, practical pursuits. You're an excellent worker, particularly if the work involves attention to detail. You apply your will quietly, with subtlety. Your sexual drive may be somewhat repressed, with the energy channeled into work. This is a good placement for work in medicine, healing, or writing.

Mars in Libra (detriment). You benefit through partnerships and express your energy best with and through other people. This placement of Mars is good for a lawyer or surgeon. Marriage may happen later in life. Your children may be gifted. You're a romantic when it comes to sex.

Mars in Scorpio (dignified). Your drive and ambition are legendary. It's difficult and sometimes downright impossible for you to compromise. Secrecy surrounds your personal projects. You make a formidable enemy and ally. Your sex drive is powerful.

Mars in Sagittarius. You have the courage to act on your convictions. This is good placement for orators, crusaders, evangelists, and New Age leaders. You have a passionate sex drive but are often impulsive and noncommittal in your relationships. It's a good sign for competitive sports, travel, and adventure.

Mars in Capricorn (exalted). Your worldly ambitions may take you into public life. You're able to plan well and to work practically to realize your ambitions and goals. You tend to keep a tight rein on your sex drive and may get involved with people who are older than you are.

Mars in Aquarius. Your unique approach may brand you as an eccentric. You act independently to achieve your goals, which are often directed toward humanity in general. Your approach to sex is apt to be rather unemotional.

Mars in Pisces. This placement can go one of two ways. You're either inconsistent in what you seek to achieve or you're able to pull together various facets of a project and make them work. Sex drive is intimately linked with emotions. This is excellent placement for a detective or occult investigator. You try to avoid conflict and confrontations.

Jupiter: Your Luck, Your Higher Mind

Philosophy. Religion. Higher education. Expansion and integration. Growth. Tradition views Jupiter as the great benefic planet, associated with luck, success, achievement, and prosperity. But it can also indicate excess, laziness, and other less desirable traits. The bottom line, though, is that Jupiter's energies are usually constructive.

This planet's energy allows us to reach out beyond ourselves and expand our consciousness. It confers a love of travel and a need to explore religious and philosophical ideas. Jupiter also allows us to integrate ourselves into the larger social order—church or religion, community, and corporation. Since Jupiter rules the abstract mind, it describes our intellectual and spiritual interests in the most profound sense.

Jupiter takes about twelve years to traverse the zodiac and averages a year in every sign. It governs publishing, the travel profession, universities and other institutions of higher learning, and traditional organized religions. Its natural houses are the ninth and the twelfth. It rules Sagittarius. Jupiter oversees the blood in general, arteries, hips, thighs, and feet (with Neptune).

Jupiter in the Signs
Jupiter in Aries. You're zealous in your beliefs and are convinced you're right, whether you are or not. Everything for you is personal and immediate. You expand your life through personal initiative, seizing opportunities when you see them or creating your own opportunities. You gain through travel, children, law, and friends.

Jupiter in Taurus. Your approach is practical. You seek to apply spiritual and philosophical principles to daily life. You gain through children and marriage and greatly love your home. Fixed in your religious or spiritual views, your generosity to others is a result of their need rather than your sympathy.

Jupiter in Gemini (detriment). The hunger for knowledge and the acquisition of information and facts expand your world. You need to communicate what you learn through writing, speaking, or maybe even film. Your travels are usually connected to your quest for understanding larger philosophical or spiritual issues. Benefits come through publishing, education, and psychic investigations.

Jupiter in Cancer (exalted). You hold onto the spiritual and moral ideals of your parents and pass these teachings down to your own children. Your spiritual beliefs are expanded through your compassion for others. Benefits come through your parents, family, and home-related matters.

Jupiter in Leo. Your beliefs are dramatized; you act on them, promote them, live them. In doing so, you attract others who help expand your world. Your exuberance, however, may be interpreted by some as outright pride. You gain through overseas trips that are connected with education, sports, or diplomatic issues.

Jupiter in Virgo (detriment). Through your work ethic and service to others, you expand your philosophical and spiritual horizons. However, your work must be purposeful. You bring a critical and analytical mind to your profession. Travel is primarily related to business. You gain through relationships with employees, and business and professional pursuits.

Jupiter in Libra. You expand your life through your associations with other people and through marriage and partnerships in general. You benefit from the opposite sex. Your sense of fair play and justice are well developed. The risk with this placement is that you may sacrifice your own interests to maintain harmony.

Jupiter in Scorpio. It's as if you were born with your spiritual beliefs already intact. You expand through your relentless search to understand these beliefs and how they relate to the nature of reality. Your willpower and determination are your greatest assets in overcoming any obstacles in your search. You gain through inheritances, psychic investigation, and any areas that Scorpio governs.

Jupiter in Sagittarius (dignified). Your deep need to understand spiritual and philosophical issues broadens your life. Travel, foreign travel in particular, and education benefit your search. This is a lucky placement for Jupiter and usually denotes success in the area described by the house in which it falls. You benefit through all things associated with Sagittarius.

Jupiter in Capricorn (in fall). Your philosophical and spiritual expansion happens mostly through your own efforts. You seek to accumulate wealth, have a great appreciation for money, and tend to be guarded in your financial generosity. You gain through your father, employers, and commercial affairs.

Jupiter in Aquarius. Your progressive views and willingness to explore all kinds of spiritual beliefs expand who and what you are. Your tolerance for other people's beliefs deepens your understanding of beliefs that differ from yours. Benefits come to you through your profession and through group associations.

Jupiter in Pisces (dignified). Your compassion, emotional sensitivity, and imagination expand your philosophical and spiritual foundations. Benefits come through psychic and occult investigations and anything to do with behind-the-scenes activities. Look toward the sign and house placement of the aspects to Pisces to find out what pushes your buttons.

Saturn: Your Responsibilities, Karma

Discipline. Responsibility. Lessons to be learned. Limitations and restrictions. Obedience. Building of foundations. No free rides. Saturn has long been known as the great malefic. While it's true that its lessons are sometimes harsh, it also provides structure and foundation, and teaches us through experience what we need in order to grow. It shows us the limitations we have and teaches us the rules of the game in this physical reality.

Astrologer Jeanne Avery, writing in *Astrology and Your Past Lives* says, "The description of Saturn's placement, aspects and rulerships in the horoscope is most important in the process of uncovering past life experiences." Even if you don't believe in reincarnation, there's ample evidence that Saturn holds a key to what the soul intends to accomplish in this life. People with a well-placed or well-aspected Saturn tend to have a practical, prudent outlook.

As one of the outer, slowly moving planets, Saturn takes twenty-nine and a half years to cross the zodiac. Its natural houses are the tenth and the eleventh. Saturn rules Capricorn. This planet governs the bones and joints, skin, and teeth.

Saturn in the Signs

Saturn in Aries (in fall). Circumstances force you to develop patience and initiative. Your impulsiveness needs to be mitigated, otherwise setbacks occur. With this position, there's a capacity for great resourcefulness which, constructively channeled, can lead to innovative creations. On the negative side, you can be self-centered and defensive.

Saturn in Taurus. You feel a deep need for financial and material security. But material comfort is earned only through hard work, discipline, and perseverance. As a result, you need to cultivate reliability and persistence in your chosen profession.

Saturn in Gemini. Discipline and structure are expressed mentally through your systematic and logical mind. Problems must be thought through carefully and worked out in detail; otherwise, difficulties multiply. You seek practical solutions.

Saturn in Cancer (detriment). Your crab-like tenacity sees you through most obstacles and difficulties. You choose a course, which may not always be the best, that doesn't threaten your emotional and financial security. There's a certain emotional restraint with this placement because so much is internalized. Psychic and intuitive resources are sometimes stifled.

Saturn in Leo (detriment). Your ego and need for recognition can be your worst enemies. If you try to solve your difficulties in a self-centered way, you only compound the problem. Cooperative ventures and consideration of mutual needs work wonders for this placement.

Saturn in Virgo. You're such a perfectionist, you tend to get bogged down in details. You need to separate the essential from the inconsequential. An intuitive approach to obstacles and challenges is an enormous help with this placement.

Saturn in Libra (exalted). You overcome obstacles and difficulties by cooperation and a willingness to work with others. The best way to achieve your goals is in partnership with others. You have the opportunity to develop an acute sense of balance and timing with this placement.

Saturn in Scorpio. You handle your difficulties in an intense, secretive manner, which increases the suspicion of those around you. By being more open and up front about what you're doing, you're able to overcome obstacles. Work to discipline your intuition; it can be an infallible guide.

Saturn in Sagittarius. You need to loosen up. Any kind of rigid approach only increases your problems and difficulties. Your best bet is to structure your life by incorporating your ideals into a practical daily life. Your intense intellectual pride makes you vulnerable to criticism by peers.

Saturn in Capricorn (dignified). No matter what challenges you face, your ambition conquers them. You know that everything has a price and strive to make your contributions to the larger world. You respect the power structures that you see. For you, life itself is serious business. Don't get locked into rigid belief systems; remain flexible.

Saturn in Aquarius (dignified). Your emotional detachment and objectivity allow you to meet challenges head on. Your innovative and unique approach to problems is best funneled through a quiet, practical application to daily life. Your peers help you to learn discipline.

Saturn in Pisces. Astrologers don't look kindly on this placement. But much of what might manifest negatively can be mitigated by practical use of the innate psychic ability of Pisces. Instead of letting yourself become trapped in memories of the past, use past triumphs as a springboard to the future. Your psychic ability is a doorway to higher spiritual truths but must be grounded in some way, perhaps through meditation or yoga.

Uranus: Your Individuality

Sudden, unexpected disruptions. Breaks with tradition and old patterns to make room for the new. Genius. Eccentricity. Astrologer Steven Forrest considers Uranus the ruler of astrology; Robert Hand calls Uranus, Neptune, and Pluto "transcendental planets" that can be dealt with constructively only with an expanded consciousness. Unless we nurture a larger perspective, Uranian disruptions appear to bring unpleasant and unexpected surprises. In reality, these disruptions liberate us, revolutionize the way we do things, and blow out the old so that the new can flow in.

In a horoscope, Uranus dictates the areas of our life in which these disruptions occur and how we utilize this energy. Do we feel it? Think about it? Seize it? Pull it deep within us so that this becomes rooted in who we are? Are we so afraid of it that we deny it? Uranus also indicates the areas in which we are most inventive, creative, and original.

This planet takes eighty-four years to go through the zodiac. Its natural house is the eleventh, and it rules Aquarius. Traditionally, before the discovery of Uranus in 1781, Saturn ruled this sign. But Saturn's rigidity just doesn't fit Aquarius. It governs electricity, inventions, the avant-garde, everything that is unpredictable or sudden.

Uranus in the Signs

Uranus in Aries. Your spirit of adventure is quite pronounced and prompts you to seek freedom at almost any price. In its most extreme form, this need for freedom can cause estrangement and a complete severance of ties with your past. You're blunt, outspoken, and can have a fiery temper. You need to develop more consideration for others.

Uranus in Taurus (in fall). You're looking for new, practical ideas concerning the use of money and financial resources, so that the old way of doing things can be reformed. You have tremendous determination and purpose. Carried to extremes, your stubbornness can impede your progress. Your materialistic attachments may limit your freedom of expression and stifle spiritual impulses.

Uranus in Gemini. Your ingenuity and intuitive brilliance impel you to pioneer new concepts in the areas where you're passionate. But your deep restlessness can make it difficult for you to follow an idea through to completion. Self-discipline will help you to bring your ideas to fruition. You travel frequently, seeking exposure to new ideas and people. You have the ability to break out of habitual living patterns and need to draw on that talent to succeed in whatever you're trying to do.

Uranus in Cancer. You pursue freedom through emotional expression and seek independence from parental authority that restricts you in some way. Your own home is unusual, either in decor or in the way you run your domestic life. There can be great psychic sensitivity with this placement, which may manifest as occult or spiritual activities in the home. This placement also carries a certain amount of emotional instability.

Uranus in Leo (detriment). Your route to freedom and independence can touch several different areas: love and romance, leadership, and the arts. Sometimes it can encompass all three. Regardless of how it manifests, you chafe at existing standards, so you create your own.

Uranus in Virgo. You have original and unique ideas regarding health, science, and technology. You seek your independence through meticulous intellectual research in whatever you undertake. There can be erratic health problems with this placement, which may spur you to look into alternative medicine and treatments.

Uranus in Libra. You seek independence through marriage and partnerships. As a result, there may be a tendency for disharmony in your personal relationships. Your unconventional ideas about law and the legal system may prompt you toward reform in that area. This placement can also produce gifted musicians.

Uranus in Scorpio (exalted). Your independence comes through drastic and profound change in whatever house Uranus in Scorpio occupies. This is an intensely emotional placement, with an innate psychic insight that allows you to perceive the nature of all that is hidden. Your temper can be quite fierce, and you may feel compelled to bring about change regardless of the consequences.

Uranus in Sagittarius. Your individuality is expressed through unique concepts in religions, philosophy, education, or spirituality. You seek out the unusual or the eccentric in foreign cultures in an attempt to incorporate other spiritual beliefs into your own. You have a deep interest in reincarnation, astrology, and other facets of the occult.

Uranus in Capricorn. This generation of people (born 1989–1994) will bring about vital changes in government and business power structures. They won't dispense with the past traditions entirely, but will restructure old ideas in new ways. Their ambitions are as strong as their desire to succeed. Look to the house placement to find out which area of life is affected.

Uranus in Aquarius (dignified). You don't hesitate to toss out old ideas and ways of doing things if they no longer work for you. You insist on making your own decisions and value judgments about everything you experience. Your independence is expressed through your impartial intellect and an intuitive sense of how to make connections between seemingly disparate issues.

Uranus in Pisces. You bring about change and seek independence through heightened intuition. You have the capacity to delve deeply into the unconscious and receive inspirations through your dreams that you can use in your daily life. Be cautious, however, that your idealism isn't impractical; face and deal with unpleasant situations as they arise.

Neptune: Your Visionary Self, Your Illusions

Hidden. Psychic. Spiritual insights. Illusions. The unconscious. This planet stimulates the imagination, dreams, psychic experiences, artistic inspiration, flashes of insight, mystical tendencies.

On the downside, it deals with all forms of escapism—drug and alcohol addiction, as well as delusion (and false idealism).

Neptune, like Uranus, overpowers Saturn's rigidity. Where Uranus disrupts the rigidity, Neptune simply negates it. This planet is considered the higher octave of Venus, and when it operates in the chart of an evolved soul, its music is extraordinary. Edgar Cayce, known as the "sleeping prophet," was such an individual. While asleep, he could diagnose physical ailments for people he'd never met, using nothing more than their names.

Neptune takes 165 years to cross the zodiac and spends about fourteen years in each sign. The twelfth house is its natural domain and it rules Pisces. It governs shipping, dance, film, and the arts in general, and is associated with mediums, clairvoyants, psychic healers, and both white and black magic.

Neptune in the Signs

Neptune in Aries. This placement fires the imagination on many levels and allows you to act on psychic impulses. Your point of illusion may be your own ego.

Neptune in Taurus. Imagination and spiritual energies are channeled into concrete expression. Your point of illusion can be your own materialism.

Neptune in Gemini. Heightened intuition bridges the left and right brain. Imagination and spiritual issues are channeled through logic and reasoning. Your blind spot may be that you believe you can take on anything. This is a sure route to burnout.

Neptune in Cancer (exalted). The enhanced psychic ability with this placement makes you impressionable. You need to be acutely aware of the fine line between illusion and reality.

Neptune in Leo. Bold, creative, and artistic concepts characterize this placement. Imagination finds expression in artistic performance. Your ego may hold you hostage.

Neptune in Virgo (detriment). Imagination and spiritual issues are carefully analyzed and fit into a broader, concrete whole for practical use. Strive not to overanalyze.

Neptune in Libra. Imagination and spiritual concepts find expression through beauty and harmony. Misplaced idealism can accompany this placement.

Neptune in Scorpio. Great imagination allows you to pierce the depth of esoteric subjects. You may be blind, however, to your own consuming interest in psychic matters. This placement can also induce drug and alcohol abuse and a sexual identity crisis.

Neptune in Sagittarius. Your intuition allows you to understand broad spiritual issues and to fit them into your personal search for truth. Your blind spot may be your need for creative freedom. In a broad, generational sense, this placement can give rise to religious cults.

Neptune in Capricorn (in fall). Spiritual ideals and concepts are given a practical structure in which to emerge. The risk lies in being so practical that the voice of the imagination is stifled.

Neptune in Aquarius. In a societal sense, heightened intuition and spiritual enlightenment bring about vast and innovative changes and discoveries under this influence. The blind spot—in terms of personal issues—is in learning to apply this energy to your own life.

Neptune in Pisces (dignified). A vivid imagination allows you to connect to deeper spiritual truths. The risk with this placement is becoming separated from reality and losing yourself in a world of illusion.

Pluto: How You Transform and Regenerate Your Life

Destiny. Transcendence. Redemption. Purge. Power. Afterlife. Good and evil. Pluto's influence is never ambivalent or passive.

Although it sometimes works in subtle ways, its repercussions in our lives are far-reaching and transformational. Its two extremes are best symbolized by Hitler and Gandhi, each man possessed of a vision that he manifested in physical reality. Both had a mission, a sense of destiny, but one caused massive destruction and the other elevated mass consciousness.

In our personal lives, Pluto's influence works in the same ways. Pluto tears down our habits and belief systems, the very structures that Saturn has helped us build, thus forcing us to transcend the ruin—or to smother in the debris.

A Pluto placement in Sagittarius, in the ninth house of philosophy and spiritual beliefs, would mean you evolve through expansion of your beliefs in these areas. But before you do, Pluto will destroy your old beliefs, collapsing them like a house of cards.

Pluto, discovered in 1930, is the most distant planet from the Sun. It exists at the very edge of our solar system—its light is so dim that Pluto seems almost etheric. It takes 248 years to complete a circuit of the zodiac. Popular astrological theory says that Pluto, like Uranus and Neptune, wasn't discovered until humanity had evolved to be able to understand its energy.

Pluto in the Signs

Pluto in Aries. It begins the reform, but doesn't have the staying power to finish what it starts. This transit will begin in 2082 and end in 2101. Perhaps the Aries pioneers will be heading out into the solar system to explore new frontiers on other planets.

Pluto in Taurus (detriment). It resists the initial change, yet slides in for the long haul once the process has started. Pluto goes into Taurus in 2101 and stays there for thirty-one years; the Taurean energy will help settle the new frontiers.

Pluto in Gemini. Regeneration manifests through the dissemination of ideas and through communication. In 2132, Pluto will go into Gemini for thirty years. New forms of communication and new ways to disseminate information will be found under this influence.

Pluto in Cancer. Regeneration comes through deep emotional involvement with the home and all that involves the home and homeland. Pluto in this sign will domesticate new worlds.

Pluto in Leo (exalted). Regeneration manifests dramatically through power struggles on an international level. The last time Pluto was in Leo, a power struggle led to World War II. Hopefully, when this transit comes around again, war will be obsolete, and Leo's power struggles will have to take place on other levels.

Pluto in Virgo. Purging occurs through a careful analysis of what is and isn't essential. Under the last transit in Virgo, great advances were made in medicine and technology. Given the rapid change in both fields, there's no telling where the next transit through Virgo may lead!

Pluto in Libra. Regeneration comes through a revamping of views toward relationships, marriages, and partnerships. By the time this transit comes around again, marriage and family may bear no resemblance at all to what they are now.

Pluto in Scorpio (dignified). This is the eleventh-hour placement of Pluto, which prevailed from 1983 to 1995. We suddenly realized that global warming wasn't just a buzzword; it's a fact. AIDS became a terrible reality. Alternative medicine became the most popular kid on the block. Gender, racial, sexual, and legal issues—everything pertinent to our survival as a society and a species—was on the evening news.

Pluto in Sagittarius. In this sign, the transformation will either succeed or fail. If it succeeds, then it's quite possible that we'll be bound as nations through our spiritual beliefs rather than our profit-and-loss statements. If it fails, chaos ensues.

Pluto in Capricorn. With typical Capricorn practicality and discipline, the pieces that Sagittarius spat out will be sculpted and molded into something useful. This will be the reconstruction period of the Aquarian Age. Kinks will be worked out, rules established.

Pluto in Aquarius (in fall). In 2041, the new order will be ready for Aquarius's humanitarian reforms.

Pluto in Pisces. This begins in 2061, nearly fifty-six years in the future. Who besides Nostradamus would presume to predict what might happen? One thing is sure, though. With Pluto in Pisces, we'll at least have a deeper understanding of who and what we are and what makes us all tick.

CHAPTER 3
READING A BIRTH CHART

A birth chart is a symbolic representation of how the heavens viewed the moment you were born. It's like a map because there is a particular way to read it and it can function as your guide. It's also a blueprint of certain personality characteristics. In this chapter you'll learn how to evaluate your own birth chart and let it guide you in your life and in your search for information about the future. Your intuition will help you do this. You can also evaluate friends' birth charts and teach them to interpret different facets of their own lives.

Signs and Symbols

Astrological signs and symbols were created for practical reasons. Consider them astrological shorthand. Once you learn about them, working with astrology and understanding astrological charts will be much easier. This understanding is important, as these charts are essential in your journey. The next three tables show the various symbols you'll become familiar with in this book.

Twelve Astrological Signs and Symbols

Sign	Symbol	Sign	Symbol
Aries	♈	Libra	♎
Taurus	♉	Scorpio	♏
Gemini	♊	Sagittarius	♐
Cancer	♋	Capricorn	♑
Leo	♌	Aquarius	♒
Virgo	♍	Pisces	♓

Planets and Symbols

Besides the Sun and the Moon, we'll be using eight planets, two nodes, and the Part of Fortune in birth charts:

Planet/Node	Symbol	Planet/Node	Symbol
Sun	☉	Saturn	♄
Moon	☾	Uranus	♅
Mercury	☿	Neptune	♆
Venus	♀	Pluto	♇
Mars	♂	North Node	☊
Jupiter	♃	South Node	☋

Aspects and Symbols

Due to the placement of planets in the houses, geometric angles are created between the planets and also between the planets and the angles of the houses. These angles are called aspects. Each aspect has a particular symbol and meaning. In this book, the following aspects are used:

Aspect	Symbol	Meaning
Conjunction	☌	A separation of 0 degrees between two or more planets
Sextile	⚹	A separation of 60 degrees between two or more planets
Square	□	A separation of 90 degrees between two or more planets
Trine	△	A separation of 120 degrees between two or more planets
Opposition	☍	A separation of 180 degrees between two or more planets

Other symbols used in a birth chart are:

- **Ascendant or Rising Sign (AS):** The sign and degree of the zodiac rising at the time of birth
- **Descendant (DS):** Opposite the ascendant, cusp of the seventh house

- **Midheaven or Medium Coeli (MC):** The highest point of the zodiac at the time of birth
- **Imum Coeli or Nadir (IC):** The zodiac point opposite the midheaven

Other symbols you'll see in the charts, but which won't be discussed in this book because they are much more complicated are:

- **Equatorial Ascendant (Eq):** The ascendant of the chart if you were born at the equator. Symbolizes who you think you are.
- **Vertex (Vtx):** A point of fate or destiny.

Rising Sign Emphasis

The ascendant (AS), or rising sign, is one of the most important features of a birth chart. Your rising sign is determined by your time of birth. The rising sign determines which planets govern the twelve houses and rules the first house of Self. It's the first of the four angles in a chart that you look at in any interpretation.

The horoscope circle is divided into twelve equal parts, numbered counterclockwise. These are the houses that represent certain types of activities and areas of life. The lines that divide the houses are called cusps. The horizontal line that cuts through the middle of the chart is the ascendant. When evaluating a birth chart, notice how planets fall in relation to the horizon or ascendant. A balanced chart has an equal number of planets above and below the horizon.

In the following birth chart, six of the ten planets are placed above the horizon. Of the four that lie under the horizon, Mars and the Moon are only one and two degrees away from the horizon (the descendant). This is close enough so that their energy is felt in the seventh house as well as the sixth. With a predominance of planets above the horizon, most experiences for this person are expressed openly. Not much is hidden. This hemisphere is concerned with conscious thought.

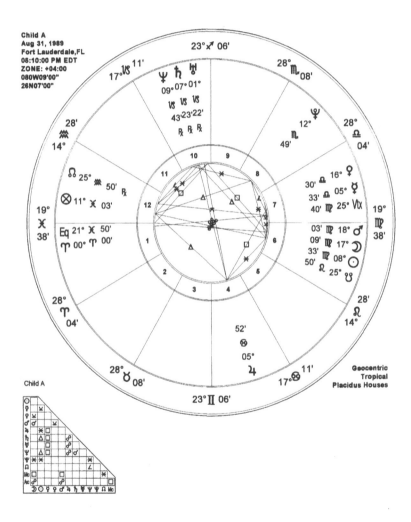

Child A

The following birth chart is almost the complete opposite of the previous one. Here, all the planets except one are under the horizon. A person with this type of placement is less obvious in what he does and more circumspect.

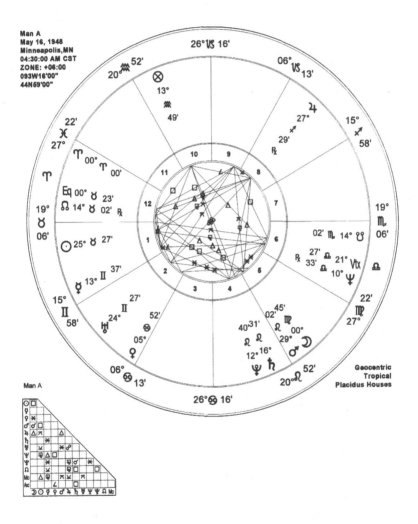

Man A
May 16, 1948
Minneapolis, MN
04:30:00 AM CST
ZONE: +06:00
093W16'00"
44N59'00"

Man A

Geocentric
Tropical
Placidus Houses

The imaginary line that divides a chart vertically is called the **MC–IC** or vertical axis. The space to the left of this axis is called the Eastern Hemisphere; this is where planets are rising. This includes houses one, two, three, ten, eleven, and twelve. The space to the right of the vertical axis is called the Western Hemisphere; this is the twilight where planets are setting. It includes houses four, five, six, seven, eight, and nine.

People with the majority of their planets to the left of the axis tend to be self-determined; they act on their own choices. Astrologer Robert Hand, however, notes: "The planets in the east should not be ones that, like Saturn, tend to frustrate action, or, like Neptune, weaken the basis on which one should act."

When a majority of the planets lie in the Western Hemisphere, an individual considers her choices before acting. Opportunities may be somewhat restricted by the society in which the person lives.

The Midheaven and the IC

The midheaven or MC is the highest point in a chart. In the first birth chart, this point is 23♐06; in the second, this point is 26♑16. The IC lies opposite the midheaven in the same degree.

Even though the midheaven doesn't provide much information about the personality, it is vital in understanding someone's life because it pertains to social roles, your public life, your relationship with authority, and status. Since it rules the cusp of the tenth house, which is concerned with an individual's professional life and career, the midheaven also helps define what a person does for a living.

Any planet that is placed closely to the cusps of the first, fourth, seventh, or tenth houses—the four angles—manifests with considerable strength. In the first chart, such planets would be Mars at 18♍03 and the Moon at 17♍09. Both are nearly conjunct the descendant or seventh house cusp. In the tenth house, Uranus at 1♑22R is within seven degrees of the midheaven at 23♄06, close enough to be particularly significant.

In the second chart, the Sun in the first house exerts a particularly strong influence.

The Houses, Defined

The sign in which a planet falls tells us how we express who and what we are. The houses explain the conditions and areas in our lives where that expression occurs. Without them, we only have part of the picture. This is what makes your birth time so important to a natal chart; the time you were born personalizes your horoscope. Otherwise, all you know are the signs of the planets that were rising and setting on your birth date.

If you don't know your time of birth, your chart can be rectified according to particular events in your life. Beginning with the ascendant, each house falls within a particular sign. That sign is governed by a particular planet, which rules that house. The planet that rules a house exerts an archetypal influence over the affairs of that house, which are interpreted as psychological and personality characteristics. In the second birth chart, Taurus lies on the ascendant so it rules the first house of Self. Since Taurus is governed by Venus, that means everything associated with the first house focuses on aesthetics, sociability, relationships, and tastes in art and literature.

In this same chart, the second house of money and material concerns falls in Gemini, ruled by Mercury. Everything that deals with second-house affairs will be colored by communication and versatility, the characteristics of Gemini and Mercury.

In traditional astrology, "angular" houses indicate action, and planets placed in these houses motivate you to action. "Succedent" houses tend to be viewed as resource houses, the things that stabilize our lives. "Cadent" houses represent diversification. But not all astrologers agree with the traditional views on the types of houses.

What the Houses Represent

Astrologers generally agree that the houses represent spheres of activity, experience, action, and areas of life impacted by the placement of planets. But they differ a bit more when it comes to how the houses are divided.

Astrologer Robert Hand notes: "At least one modern writer has proposed a twenty-four house system. And the Irish sidereal astrologer Cyril Fagan has unearthed ancient references to the *oktotopos,* an eightfold division numbered clockwise form the Ascendant instead of counterclockwise as we are used to." The situation becomes especially muddled when you toss in the ancient Greek traditions and modern Hindu astrology.

The trick is to work with the traditional meanings, then allow your intuition to guide you. You may find, for instance, that you read the mother in the tenth house and the father in the fourth; or that in the horoscope for a man, the mother is in the fourth but for a woman, the father is in the fourth. The point is to develop a system that works for you by studying your own chart first.

As you delve into your own chart and the charts of family and friends, you'll develop your own opinions on what the houses mean and how they should be grouped. For now, try to stick to the traditional meanings. Here is a list of keywords for the twelve houses:

- **House 1:** *Personality.* The Self, beginnings, physical health, early life, physical appearance
- **House 2:** *Finances.* Personal material resources, assets, expenditures, attitudes toward money
- **House 3:** *Communication.* Intellect and mental attitudes, short journeys, brothers and sisters, neighbors, relatives
- **House 4:** *Home.* Family life, domestic affairs, mother or father, early childhood conditioning, your roots, the end of your life, real estate

- **House 5:** *Children and Creativity.* Pleasurable pursuits, creative outlets, children (the firstborn in particular), love affairs, sex for pleasure
- **House 6:** *Work and Health.* Working conditions and environment, competence and skill, general health
- **House 7:** *Partnerships and Marriage.* Partnerships in general, marriage, open conflicts, our identification with others
- **House 8:** *Death and Inheritances, the Occult.* Transformation of all kinds, regeneration, sexuality, taxes, death, psychic ability
- **House 9:** *Higher Mind.* Philosophy and religion, law, long journeys, higher education, publishing, foreign travel and interests, ambitions, in-laws and relatives of the marriage partner
- **House 10:** *Career.* Profession, status, mother or father, worldly ambitions, public life, people in power over you, status
- **House 11:** *Friends.* Group associations, hopes and wishes, ambitions and goals, your network of friends
- **House 12:** *Personal Unconscious.* Institutions, confinement, that which we haven't integrated into ourselves, karma

A Look at Each House

If you operate from the premise that the soul chooses all facets of the circumstances into which it is born, then your chart becomes the voice of your soul speaking to you. Since there are twelve houses, and each house is well defined in the coming pages, you need to study your chart to find out about your predispositions, talents, affinities, and behavior, as well as about those who you partner well with, are drawn toward, and can rely on. Read on.

First House (Ascendant): Your Mask
Natural sign: Aries
Natural ruler: Mars

All of us are mixtures of intellectual and emotional needs, talents, memories, desires, dreams, fears, and triumphs. These characteristics are streamlined and rolled into our personalities, the face we present to others, our masks. The first house is our social mask.

This house ruled by the ascendant also governs our physical appearance and the general state of our physical health. The head and face are governed by the first house. (When looking for health issues in a chart, always look to the first house, as well as to the sixth and the eighth.) In this house, the source of illness can be due to an inability to impact the world in the way or to the degree that we want. Consider the following descriptions of the ascendant in each of the signs as personality signatures.

Aries. People under this sign have a need to succeed at everything they take on. They're impulsive, impatient, driven, fiercely independent, and decisive.

Taurus. People under this sign are marked by determination, patience, practicality, and appreciation of beauty. It takes a lot to anger them, but once they're provoked, watch out! People with Taurus rising are often physically attractive and identifiable by short, strong necks.

Gemini. People under this sign need versatility and diverse experiences. These people are mentally quick and perceptive. They are often slender, with long arms and fingers, and walk quickly.

Cancer. People under this sign drive to establish some sort of foundation or home base that defines who they are. They're intuitive and capable of deep feeling. With Cancer rising, the face is often round. They tend toward stoutness in middle age.

Leo. Think drama, pride, and ambition with this rising sign. People under this sign have an excellent ability to organize and direct others, and understand children very well. Physically, these people are handsome and large-boned with thick, beautiful hair.

Virgo. People under this sign possess keen powers of observation and have a fastidious nature. They generally are dedicated to service of others, have a concern for health, and can be very intuitive. Slender bodies and oval faces with a certain softness and charm mark these people.

Libra. People under this sign define themselves through social relationships. They seek harmony and fairness in all they undertake and often are so concerned with being fair that they are indecisive. Physically, Libra rising often produces nearly perfectly formed bodies and physical beauty.

Scorpio. Born under this sign, these people exhibit intensity, passion, strong sexuality, and a profound perception into the secret nature of life. They are deeply intuitive and possess the ability to drastically alter their personal environment. They tend to have dark hair that is wavy and thick and prominent brows.

Sagittarius. These people have an adventurous spirit, bluntness in speech, and deep independence. They have excellent foresight, a respect for all spiritual thought, and a love of animals. Their bodies are usually tall and slender, with a stoop to the shoulders.

Capricorn. They're concerned about status, self-discipline, and ambition. Impulsive activity is generally restrained. They're good at recognizing and defining the overall structure of a problem or challenge. Physically they can be thin and bony, with prominent features.

Aquarius. They are humanitarians, and also possess unusual or eccentric modes of self-expression. People with this rising sign tend to go against the established order and seek their own truths. They have strong, well-formed bodies, with a tendency to plumpness in middle age.

Pisces. Few rising signs possess more emotional sensitivity and profound perception. People under this sign are often mystically inclined and impressionable, with multifaceted self-expression. They have exquisitely shaped hands and feet and usually have compelling eyes.

Second House: Your Material Goods
Natural sign: Taurus
Natural ruler: Venus

If the planets are aspects to the ascendant and the first house creates issues about self-esteem and self-doubt, the second house can be where we attempt to work them out. This can manifest in any type of behavior that draws attention to our personal material resources. In other words, our self-doubt impels us to prove our own worth through money and possessions.

Third House: Your Mind
Natural sign: Gemini
Natural ruler: Mercury

A lot of issues are lumped into this house: the intellect, communication, brothers and sisters, short journeys, conscious thinking, neighbors, and relatives. But this house actually represents daily activities in our lives, things we do automatically. The mental energy is analytical.

A short journey is a commute to work as opposed to a trip to Europe. Brothers, sisters, neighbors, and relatives refer to our experience of these people, not with the people themselves. It implies an unconscious ease that exists between people who have something in common, whether it's genes or the street they live on.

Fourth House (IC): Your Roots
Natural sign: Cancer
Natural ruler: Moon

This house symbolizes emotional and physical security. For all of us, this begins with our family, homes, parents, and our sense of belonging.

Some discrepancy exists among astrologers as to whether the fourth house represents the mother or the father. It is often used to symbolize the primary nurturing parent; the primary provider and authoritarian figure is found in the tenth house. Over the course of a lifetime parents often exchange roles, but generally one will be more nurturing and the other more authoritarian. In later life, this house indicates how we support others.

In the fourth house, we also find issues related to real estate, the collective unconscious, and information regarding the last twenty years or so of a person's life.

Fifth House: Your Pleasures
Natural sign: Leo
Natural ruler: Sun

Pleasure is the core meaning of the fifth house, but because pleasure is something different to all of us, this can include creativity, children, love affairs, sex, gambling, meditating, running, parties, a nature walk, celebrations, gazing at a piece of art, or reading a book.

The children part of this house also refers to the act of creating them. In this sense, Saturn placed here can indicate a possible stillbirth, abortion, or miscarriage, possibly involving the firstborn. But it can just as easily indicate a restriction or limitation on the pursuit of pleasure—someone too serious to have fun. The interpretation would depend on whose chart you're reading and the aspects to the house.

Sixth House: Health and Work
Natural sign: Virgo
Natural ruler: Mercury

Centuries ago, one of the definitions of this house concerned servants: handmaidens, stable boys, cooks, and maids—in other words, the chattel. In today's world it refers to the way we extend ourselves for others, and the services we perform without any thought of remuneration. It also refers to our general work conditions.

Health issues are also included here. But the illnesses associated with the sixth house are often linked to your work or job. Anything that stifles growth and self-expression—overwork, despising what you do, working just to pay the bills—can lead to illness.

Ultimately, the illness may trigger a transformation in consciousness that forces you to take a vacation, quit your dead-end job, or re-evaluate what you're doing. When that happens, health and hygiene awareness usually increases. In the healing period, it's important to follow your own intuition.

Seventh House (Descendant): Partnerships
Natural sign: Libra
Natural ruler: Venus

This house is about marriage and close partnerships of all kinds. It concerns how you relate to a significant other and how, in doing so, you often deal with an unexpressed aspect of yourself.

When you love someone, you identify with that person. This is the kind of intimate relationship the seventh house addresses—a relationship that implies commitment. It can also refer to business partnerships where a commitment is made.

Eighth House: Your Instincts
Natural sign: Scorpio
Natural ruler: Pluto and Mars

This house is loaded. It's obsessed with death, sex, and taxes—with the occult tossed in just to muddle things. More specifically, it also includes death benefits, insurance, the partner's earning capacity, alimony, joint finances of any kind, and the recycling of goods.

Traditionally, it's known as the house of death. If that strikes you as bleak, then think of the eighth house as one of transformation. Death is one kind of transformation; sexuality is another; psychic and occult matters are yet another. The house is emotionally loaded because it deals with issues that most of us don't like to dwell on. This emotional impact, however, is why eighth-house events often feel fated or destined. This house relates to the internal energy that seeks outward growth, expansion, and experience.

Ninth House: Higher Mind
Natural sign: Sagittarius
Natural ruler: Jupiter

As the opposite of the third house, the ninth concerns higher ideals, the higher mind, philosophy, religion and spirituality, the law, foreign cultures, and long journeys. Through the ninth house we seek to understand the whole picture and our place in it. We reach out to experience and then try to assimilate the experience into a worldview, a belief system. This can be done through reading, education, and travel—all ninth-house pursuits.

Tenth House (Midheaven): External Achievements
Natural sign: Capricorn
Natural ruler: Saturn

Where the sixth house covers what you do to earn a living, the tenth concerns your career or profession, work that provides a social role in the larger world. It's the work with which we identify ourselves and by which others identify us.

Clerical work, for instance, probably falls into the sixth house unless the individual identifies closely with the job. But if the clerical worker is a nationally known antique car collector who identifies and is identified in that field, then this would fall into the tenth house. This house also represents the authoritarian parent as well as our experience of authority figures.

Eleventh House: Friends and Ambitions
Natural sign: Aquarius
Natural ruler: Uranus

This house is about manifestation, about the power of manifestation through a group or collective consciousness. It took me a long time to understand this.

In the eleventh house, we don't just get along with certain types of people; there are some people with whom we click immediately. Part of their belief system overlaps and parallels our own. With these people, we have an especially strong affinity and from this affinity rises a certain kind of power: the group of collective mind, the mind that works toward a common end, a shared ideal, and a particular goal.

Signs and planets in this house offer clues about the types of friends and associations that not only benefit us but also whom we might benefit as well. As astrologer Steven Forrest writes: "Establish goals. Find people who support them. Then live in the present moment. That is the secret of successful eleventh-house navigation."

Twelfth House: Your Personal Unconscious
Natural sign: Pisces
Natural ruler: Neptune

This house is typically considered to be negative and dark, the psychic garbage pail of the zodiac. In medieval times, it was known as the house of troubles and indicated possibilities of imprisonment, illness, secret enemies, poverty, and dire misfortune. While such possibilities exist with this house, its core meaning is deeper.

The twelfth house represents the personal unconscious, the parts of ourselves that we've disowned—all that is hidden from our conscious perception. Here lie the dregs of early defeats and disillusionments, which ultimately were repressed and not integrated into the rest of our personality. Here, too, are aspects of ourselves that for one reason or another we don't want to express openly to others. These hidden parts of ourselves often come out later in life, surfacing as fears, weaknesses, or phobias that work against us.

Sometimes, these repressed aspects find expression in our most intimate relationships. The daughter of an alcoholic parent, for instance, may find herself confronting her childhood experiences in her relationship with an alcoholic spouse.

On a higher level, the twelfth house can embody spiritual, psychic, and mystical experiences that deepen our connection with the divine.

Evaluating and Interpreting Your Chart

When evaluating the house in a chart, you should have certain guidelines in mind. Consider the following:

1. Note the ascendant. What element is it in? What does the sign immediately tell you about the individual? Where does the ruling planet fall?
2. Note the cusps of the fourth house (the **IC**), the seventh house (the descendant), and the cusp of the tenth (the midheaven or **MC**). What do these signs immediately tell you about the person? What do the planets in these houses tell you about the person?
3. What houses do the Sun and the Moon occupy? Are they above or below the horizon? In the Western or the Eastern Hemispheres? In which elements?
4. Note any house where there's a cluster of planets. A house that holds more than one planet indicates activity in that area. It holds a clue as to the soul's purpose in life.
5. Are there any houses that hold three or more planets within three degrees of each other? This cluster is called a *stellium*

and indicates intensely focused activity in that particular house.

6. Which house holds the Part of Fortune? Where are the Moon's nodes? The placement of these three points provides valuable information about the soul's purpose.

7. Does the chart have a singleton, one planet that stands alone? An example is in the first birth chart given in this chapter, with Jupiter sticking up there all alone in the eighth house.

8. What intuitive feelings do you get from the chart?

9. What is the chart's general shape?

When you have a birth chart in front of you, allow your intuition the freedom to make connections you might not perceive with your conscious mind. Sometimes, those connections are the only ones that matter to the other person. Don't allow the science part of astrology to become dogma. Learn the basics, assimilate them, and then let your intuition speak to you.

When you intuit something, you feel a "click" or an "aha" as you experience it. It's like following a hunch, and it just feels right. The sensation is different for everyone, but it does seem to register somewhere in the body while it's happening. It may be a tightening in your stomach, a sudden pulsing at your temple, or a flash of heat in your hands and fingertips. Once you experience it, you never forget it. Remember to follow your intuition after you have all the facts. It won't let you down.

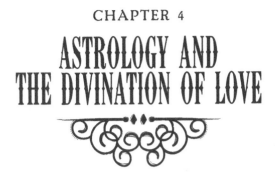

CHAPTER 4

ASTROLOGY AND THE DIVINATION OF LOVE

Love compatibility is a tricky thing. On the one hand, there are so many obvious matches, but some supposed mismatches work, too. It's difficult to know everything from a couple's set of Sun signs. However, Sun signs will give you a basic idea of whether or not you'll get along as a couple. In this chapter, find out more about the various signs and their idea of love. Check out the "Matches" section of each sign for some big hints.

Aries in Love

Aries man has a penchant for doing things his way. He's as sharp as a tack and people respect him, even though they think he's bossy and domineering. He'll decide how he wants it done, and he's a perfectionist about it. If he likes you, he'll listen to your take on it, and perhaps tailor it a bit. But if he doesn't like you, watch out! There is no better debater than Aries. He must win every argument—even when he's wrong.

Aries woman, on the other hand, handles people with more charm and finesse. She's a lot less aggressive than Aries man—on the outside—though her thought process is very similar. Where he drives forward, she'll pull back and wait for the masses to come to her—and they always do. When it comes to love, she's just as fickle and stubborn as Aries man.

Matches with Aries

Here's the kicker: If you want a faithful Aries, try to stay away from those who have their Venus (their love sign) in Aries, Sagittarius, or even Aquarius. They tend to wander. If you're an Earth sign, pick an Aries with lots of Air in his chart—he'll be drawn to you. If you're a Water sign, you'll probably do well with Aries if he has a lot of Fire.

And if you want an Aries who lives for love, find an Aries with his Venus in Cancer or Pisces. Aries, because it's a Fire sign, is often attracted to other Fire signs—Sagittarius or Leo. But generally, unless aspects in the chart indicate otherwise, romance with another Fire sign can be explosive. Aries gets along well with Air signs—Gemini, Libra, Aquarius—or a sign that's sextile (60 degrees) or trine (120 degrees) from Aries. Sometimes, an Earth sign helps ground all that Aries energy. In chart comparisons, a Venus or Moon in Aries in the other person's chart would indicate compatibility.

Leo in Love

Leos are passionate. They can also be impulsive and irrational, but it's all part of the charm. They're fickle, and they like to test their partners before they put their hearts into anything. They're difficult, too, particularly when their egos need to be stroked. If you treat a Leo with anything but the ultimate respect, he may not say anything, but he'll remember it—and count it against you in the game of love.

Leo fights for the underdog, but be sure to stick up for yourself with him. On the other hand, arguing for the sake of arguing will make a Leo insane. Leos are intense and will argue, but their sunny, calm natures are truly made for being content and feeling safe and comfortable with a partner.

If you make a Leo feel secure, he'll be more likely to fall in love with you. And making him secure doesn't mean making yourself a doormat. Let Leo know he can be himself with you—that you won't judge him—and he'll relax in your presence and show his true colors.

For the most part, Leos need to feel needed and need to know they are loved before they commit entirely. Once they're committed, everything is bigger than life and brighter than the Sun. They're known to be loyal, but this is only true after they've found themselves. If they haven't, and they're not yet emotionally evolved or secure, they can be as two-faced as Gemini can be.

Many astrologers say Leos are arrogant, but this is not true. Actually, they're such perfectionists that they're worried their insecurities will show unless they "perform." They show off sometimes and try to be larger than life to compensate for their flaws.

Matches with Leo

Another Fire sign is good for a Leo simply because their energy levels are similar. Any sign that is sextile (Gemini, for instance) or trine (Aries) would be fine, too—though Leo has little patience for Aries who aren't spiritually evolved. True, he may win her for a while, but then what? He can be too head-strong. Aries is a lot like Sagittarius with Leo—lots of fire, but not the same temperament. Sagittarius can be a bit too wise and quiet (or even too superficial or stubborn) for Leo; Aries can be too demanding and controlling.

The polarity between Leo and Aquarius, its polar opposite sign, may elevate a Leo's consciousness to where it succeeds best—to the wider world beyond himself, if the Leo has some Air signs in his chart. Capricorn can be an interesting match and Scorpio seems like a go until Leo realizes that she may not like the way he may raise their children. But they're surely a good match in bed.

Sagittarius in Love

Sagittarius is pretty clear in what he wants. He knows if he's in love—truly—or not. It's simply not a question. "Making" a Sagittarius fall in love is difficult. You can play a little hard to get in the beginning, and this will help, but, ultimately, Sagittarius is instinctive and wise—and knows what he needs.

He's so blunt and tactless with his words that they can sometimes cut to the core. But believe everything that comes out of a Sagittarian's mouth. If he tells you he's in love, he is. If he tells you he's not, he's not. Sagittarius is not a very diplomatic soul. In his mind, honesty and straightforwardness is everything, and he likes someone who will listen carefully to everything he has to say.

Strangely enough, Sagittarius sometimes gives the impression that he's lost in another world. He seems quiet—or into himself. This isn't entirely true. It always seems that Sagittarius is deeper than he really is. In truth, he's probably thinking about work or some kind of problem in quantum physics—he's not thinking about your relationship.

Sagittarius wants everything to go smoothly. In his mind, if things are not moving forward, he's not going to waste his precious time devoting it to you. Just don't badger him for his thoughts. Let Sagittarius come to you to ask you how you're feeling. He needs to be left alone to experience his space and freedom, and then he'll come search you out.

Matches with Sagittarius

Other Air signs are compatible with Sagittarius. The Sagittarius-Gemini polarity confers a natural affinity between the two signs. But other Fire signs might work well, too. It just depends. Sagittarius, above all other Fire signs, is the most emotionally secure. Sagittarius is not the most stable (Leo is), but he thinks he is. This can make him a bit of a know-it-all. He doesn't tolerate as much as Leo, but he's not as ridiculously immature as Aries can sometimes be.

He comes off as a natural, quiet leader. And he is. Actually, the best match for Sagittarius is a Water sign—particularly Pisces. These two go together so well because Pisces is strong and sensual enough for Sagittarius, but is also a master in the art of silent persuasion. Sagittarius needs someone who is loving, sweet, and tender, will let him do what he feels like doing, and isn't nitpicky about the little things. Again, a Water sign might just do him good because he likes being "shown the way;" yet, all the while, he's the one who can act "in charge" of things.

Gemini in Love

The problem with Gemini is that he doesn't really know what he wants. He thinks he knows, but then it changes. Gemini needs to work for love—then he'll give his all. Also, he needs a partner who makes him laugh—but not about himself. Geminis can be touchy and sensitive when the humor comes at their expense.

Geminis love first with their minds. Even a relationship that begins primarily because of a sexual attraction won't last if there's no mental connection. Quite often, Geminis seek friendship first with the opposite sex and, once a mental rapport is established, the friendship deepens into love. But this happens when they're really ready for something serious. Otherwise, they can have affairs like no other sign in the zodiac. True, they can be quite fickle in their affections, sometimes carrying on simultaneous relationships. But once their hearts are won, they love deeply.

Again, Geminis give great advice, though they're just not very good at taking the advice themselves. So, they're a little lost. And they change their minds frequently, so it's sometimes difficult for them to get to the heart of the matter. All of that aside, Geminis do love with every bit of their hearts. They're pretty quick to put their hearts on the table when they feel it—sometimes too quickly. They can be diplomatic when they need to—but not when it comes to romance, love, and you.

Matches with Gemini

Geminis are social enough to get along with and be attracted to just about anyone on a superficial basis. They feel most at home with other Air signs, particularly Aquarians, whose minds are as quick as theirs. They also get along with Sagittarius, their polar opposites in the zodiac, who share some of the same attributes. Again, though, these are broad generalizations. For compatibility purposes, it's important to compare the individual charts.

When Gemini is truly ready to settle down, an Earth sign may be a good option for a partner. A Virgo will be a bit too critical for the thin-skinned Gemini, but a Taurus, with his feisty sensual side, may just be what the doctor ordered. Capricorn can go either way, but most Capricorns won't put up with Gemini's otherwise flighty antics or superficial skimming of political ideas that hold great truths for Capricorns.

Again, an Air sign like Libra may be ideal for Gemini if they can find a balance of minds. If anyone can find that rare balance, it's Libra. The only problem is that Libra despises confrontation and Gemini tends to go that way. Water signs are probably too side-stepping for feisty Gemini—unless they have a lot of Earth or Air in their charts. Scorpio and Gemini are a good match in bed, but Scorpio sometimes weighs Gemini down when he wants to go out and play. Leo can be a fun dating partner for Gemini—with a lot of laughter—but Leo may get annoyed when Gemini doesn't praise the ground she walks on. If Gemini does, it's a match made in heaven.

Libra in Love

Libras are drawn to beauty, whatever its form. The only thing they enjoy as much as beauty is harmony. Even when a relationship has gone sour, a Libra hesitates to be the one who ends it. Libras can't stand hurting anyone's feelings; emotional rawness is one of those ugly realities that they don't like to see. As a result, they may remain in a relationship longer than they should just because disharmony is so distasteful. Libras seek harmony because, in their hearts, they know that enlightenment lies at the calm dead center of the storm.

In fact, Libra is just that—the eye of the storm. He'll start something and then walk away to watch things unfold at a distance, where it's safe. Libra is the ultimate "watcher" of human behavior. He studies it—studies you—and determines what he knows and what he believes from that. He'll have his friends study you and see if you're faithful and "worthy." Ultimately, he'll make up his own mind. But if a Libra doesn't trust you, you're history. He'll never put the time in to get to know you.

It seems as if Libra has many friends. True, he has a wonderful social circle and many people who believe in him. But watch closely. Libra keeps his true self hidden from the world. There's usually only one person he truly trusts—usually a family member. If he opens up to you completely on a consistent basis, you've got a real mate for life.

Librans are masters in the disguise of their own fate. In fact, they can be very stubborn when deciding what the roads of life all lead to. It's sometimes difficult for them to make a tough decision, but when they do, no one can talk them out of it. Librans believe in signs, red flags, and even superstitions. They'll consider omens and apply them to their own lives.

Also, Librans want to be calm and comfortable in a relationship. Many Libra men choose younger women just to have this feeling of ultimate control. Sometimes they also pick women a lot older than they are so that the woman does all of the deciding. You'll also find that Librans are mostly faithful when they find the one they want to spend time with. True, they may have strange arrangements set up, but when they love, they love deeply.

Matches with Libra

Librans can get along with just about anyone. They are most compatible with other Air signs, Aquarius and Gemini. Though seriously outgoing, Geminis can sometimes scare them—they understand the way Librans think. Scorpios get to the heart of the matter with Libra; they have the intensity and emotional depth that Librans crave. In fact,

Librans might even get attached to Scorpios in a volatile and unhealthy way, if they're not careful. Though Scorpios can be a good match for Libras, they should watch out for signs of control. If Librans feel they're being manipulated in any way, they'll be out the door in a flash.

Librans also gravitate toward people who reflect their refined tastes and aesthetic leanings, like Leo. Also, an Earth sign may provide a certain grounding that a Libran needs. Taurus is a wonderful, sensual match with Libra. Or a Water sign, like Cancer, may offer a fluidity of emotion that a Libran may lack. But, with Cancer, it may be an uphill battle. Cancers can be too moody, sometimes, and too self-involved for harmony-seeking Librans.

Since opposites attract, Aries can sometimes be a good fit for Librans—though Aries needs to have spiritually "found herself" before this can work. On another note, a Libra with a Libra can be a good match—but watch out! Two of the same signs together can be wonderful or a big mess.

Aquarius in Love

Aquarians need the same space and freedom in a relationship that they crave in every other area of their lives. Even when they commit, the need doesn't evaporate. They must follow the dictates of their individuality above all else. This stubbornness can work against them if they aren't careful. Aquarians usually are attracted to people who are unusual or eccentric in some way. Their most intimate relationships are marked by uniqueness.

Aquarians can be very instinctive but usually for other people, not for themselves. They also try to root for the underdog, but sometimes pick the wrong underdog or victim to defend. Their upbeat, positive outlook on life can be tempered by idealistic notions they try hard to suppress. The biggest goal in life, for them, is to remain calm and cool. This is very important for Aquarius because, when they let loose, they can be big fireballs. And, if they get too wound up, the aggression they exude can be harsh for other people to cope with. Instinctively, they know this and try to temper it, often unsuccessfully.

Aquarians know that they're strong individuals and that they can turn the tides to their favor. Luck follows them everywhere—even if they're not aware of it. There's something of a destined feeling to the relationships of Aquarians. They may even sense where they're headed before the fact. An Aquarius is not a big mystery, though. If you want an answer about love, just ask. Aquarians will tell you if your relationship is headed somewhere or not. If they're not sure, chances are that the answer is no, but they can be swayed over time.

Aquarius also must see a bit of the world before settling down. He plays a little game with himself. He may even get married a couple of times before realizing that he just wasn't ready for what he thought he was. An ideal partner for Aquarius will show his own mental agility, his independence, and his emotional strength of will. This will get an Aquarius to follow you to the ends of the earth, but only if he's ready for something real to enter his life.

Matches with Aquarius

Due to the lack of prejudice in this sign, Aquarians usually get along with just about everyone. They're particularly attracted to people with whom they share an intellectual camaraderie—someone who makes them laugh and makes them feel good about themselves. In this way, Gemini can be a fabulous match for Aquarius, as long as they don't butt heads. This relationship can work only if the two find balance between neediness and independence. Also, Gemini can be extremely jealous and possessive with mates, which Aquarius abhors.

Many Aquarians wind up with Virgos. Virgos have the kind of stubbornness and organized stability that Aquarians secretly crave. But this may also be an ego thing. Remember, Aquarius loves a challenge and Virgo keeps them squirming with their moral lectures and hardheaded ways. But, mentally and in bed, these two can do very well together.

A Libra or another Aquarius can be a good match—especially if one is more outgoing and gregarious than the other and lets his partner shine. This is a good example of two of the same (Air) signs doing well together. Aquarians are usually secure enough to see bad and good traits in a partner that are similar to their own, and still be able to deal with it and move ahead with the relationship.

A sign that's sextile or trine to Aquarius will also work. And Aquarius's polar opposite, Leo, can be an interesting mate for Aquarius. If Aquarius doesn't get too self-involved and gives Leo her fair due, this can work. But Leo is usually running after Aquarius, and Aquarius can get bored of that—fast. If Leo pulls away a little, this rapport can function well. All in all, Aquarius is a great partner if you've truly won his heart. If not, you'll just be a stop along the way for lively Aquarius, who craves adventure and experience.

Cancer in Love

Cancers can be evasive when it comes to romance. They flirt coyly, yet all the while they're feeling their way through the maze of their own emotions. It's true. Astrologers will tell you that Cancers feel deeply; but what they don't tell you is that Cancers are also very good at putting their feelings "on hold." In other words, if they're not already in love with you, they can pull back and see the relationship for what it is at a distance.

On the other hand, if they're in love, it's not so easy for them to let go. They tend to go the cheating route to push away a partner rather than fess up and just say how they feel. In fact, beware of Cancers dodging questions and important issues. They find it difficult to open up and talk about their true, personal feelings. If they do, with you, you've got an edge over all the others. Once again the whole "side-stepping" part of Cancer is absolutely true. True to their crab sign, they mimic the crustacean with surprising accuracy.

Just remember: to live with and love a Cancer, you have to accept the intensity of their emotions. It's a war they have within themselves, and they'll want to embroil you in it. Unfortunately, they're too busy taking care of you and others to know (and show) what's eating at them. You'll have to get to the heart of the matter yourself.

Matches with Cancer

On the surface, Pisces, as the other dreamy Water sign, would seem to be the most compatible with a Cancer. But Pisces's all-over-the-map sense of style with Cancer's sidestepping could be frustrating for both. Plus, the duality of Pisces would, most likely, drive a Cancer person crazy. One of the best combinations here is Water sign Scorpio. Cancer manages Scorpio with bravado and knows how to get the ever-changing Scorpio hooked. A little mystery goes a long way with Scorpio, and, in the case of this match, Cancer cannot help but induce a little intrigue with her onslaught of bottled-up emotions that lie just beneath the surface. Scorpio might just bring it out of Cancer.

Earth signs—Taurus, Virgo, and Capricorn—are particularly good for Cancers, especially Taurus and Virgo because they are sextile to Cancer. Fire signs with Cancer, on the other hand, tend to bring out the worst in Cancer—unless it's, perhaps, a very evolved Fire sign. In rare cases, Leos do well with Cancers (especially if the Leo is the man).

Scorpio in Love

You don't know the meaning of the word intensity unless you've been involved with a Scorpio. No other sign brings such raw power to life. The rawness probably isn't something you understand or even like very much, but there's no question that it's intricately woven through the fabric of your relationship.

The odd part is that you're never quite sure how the intensity is going to manifest: jealousy, fury, endless questions, or soft and intriguing, but affective passion. Sometimes, the intensity doesn't have anything to do with the relationship, but with the personal dramas in the Scorpio's life. Many times, you may even hear from work colleagues that he's a "perfectionist, and difficult to work with." The word "crazy" may even get into the picture, so don't try to figure it out.

Scorpios have a magnetism that is legendary. It doesn't even matter if he's good-looking—it's always there. Consider this: Scorpio is always the sexiest person in the room. Astrologers say that Scorpio is also known for his bedroom prowess: this isn't myth. Unfortunately, other problems can weigh Scorpio down so he's got to be clear of mind and calm in order to woo you in his cool, mysterious way.

Scorpio's senses are strong, especially those of sight, touch, and taste. If he touches you, you'll feel it down to your toes. He has keen sight, meaning instincts. And taste: if he cooks, he's wonderful. If not, he appreciates everything about food. However, there's one sense he lacks: hearing. It seems as if he doesn't hear anything you say. It's not that he doesn't really remember. Instead, he has a mental block on the things he doesn't want to address, or he's very likely to pretend he doesn't know what you're talking about. The truth is, Scorpios have excellent memories. Don't let him get away with this.

Matches with Scorpio

Scorpio is usually compatible with Taurus, because the signs are polar opposites and balance each other. The Water of Scorpio and the Earth of Taurus mix well. However, both signs are fixed, which means that in a disagreement neither will give in to the other. Scorpios can be compatible with other Scorpios as long as each person understands the other's intensity and passions. Pisces and Cancer, the other two Water signs, may be too weak for Scorpio's intensity, unless a comparison of natal charts indicates otherwise.

Fire signs may blend well with Scorpio, depending on their charts. If a Scorpio is emotionally solid, a Leo may be a good match. Scorpio loves Leo's sunny nature, and is drawn to it. If

Scorpio doesn't pull Leo down with him, this can work okay. Sagittarius, especially if Scorpio is near the cusp of Sagittarius, can be the same—but ditto with the "bringing her down with the house." If the two can respect each other and find a good balance, this can work. Aries and Scorpio, however, will find that the emotional gap is probably too much of a chasm to cross.

Pisces in Love

Through the heart, sensitive Pisces experiences his subjective reality as real, solid, perhaps even more tangible than the external world. For some Pisces, romance can be the point of transcendence—the source where he penetrates to the larger mysteries that have concerned him most of his life. To be romantically involved with a Pisces is to be introduced to many levels of consciousness and awareness. If you're not up to it, then get out now because your Pisces isn't going to change

There is nothing weak about Pisces, as many astrologers claim. Instead, Pisces watches from a distance and determines the best point of attack. Pisces, also, many times seems the quiet type, who's sweet and kind. But know this: when Pisces is in a relationship, and feels comfortable, there is no one who can manipulate you and your feelings like Pisces can (except, maybe, Cancer). The way a Pisces does this is to play cold and walk away until you follow. Pisces knows that this always works in human nature and has this move down to a science.

He's strong because he'll get you to come to him without any effort on his part. Pisces are ten times craftier than they appear. They're incredibly good at hiding this side of themselves. They're so adept at playing along with you, and being "on your side," that you won't even know what hit you when they use something—something you've told them—against you in the future.

They say Pisces is idealistic. This is true. But they also say that Pisces is a dreamer, and there is a misconception about this. Yes, Pisces is a dreamer: but he's a dreamer with a vision. Most Pisces know what they want and go after it with a kind of slow, methodical gait. Eventually, most of them get what they want, even if it takes time. But Pisces instinctively know how best to get the most out of their astonishingly calm composure and patience.

There is no one like Pisces to give you good advice. Aries may be good at it, but he orders you around while doing so. His words are more command and "truth" than suggestion. Gemini is good at it, but usually comes up with the overly aggressive way. Instead, Pisces will put the idea into your head and let you come up with the solution. This is, indeed, most effective and one of Pisces's best traits.

Matches with Pisces

Other Water signs seem the obvious choice here. But Scorpio might overpower Pisces and Cancer might be too clingy. The signs sextile to Pisces are Capricorn and Taurus. While Capricorn might be too limited and grounded for the Piscean imagination, Taurus probably fits right in. Gemini, because it's a mutable sign like Pisces, can be compatible.

The shocker here is that Sagittarius may just be the best combination for Pisces. Though they're such opposites, they complement each other quite well. Pisces is able to soothe the Sagittarius savage beast—and they fit like two pieces of a puzzle. Pisces also lets Sagittarius do what he wants, yet always keeps the upper hand with a cool, polished, quietly strong demeanor. And this is what Sagittarius likes best. As for the other Fire signs, there doesn't seem to be much chance, but it truly depends on the other factors in the two separate charts.

Taurus in Love

In romance with a Taurus, a lot goes on beneath the surface. Taureans are subtle and quiet about what they feel. Once they fall, though, they fall hard. In fact, their inherent fixed natures simply won't allow them to give up. Perhaps this sounds like it could be good for you and bad for them. Maybe. But Taurus people get in way over their heads and then find that there's no turning back.

However, a Taurus will never really fall in love unless he thinks he can trust you. Trust definitely goes a long way with Taurus. Deep down, Taurus knows that he's sensitive and that he takes himself a little too seriously. His sense of responsibility weighs heavily on his shoulders and he'll always fulfill any task he believes he must.

But, remember: he'll also feel like it's up to him to judge the world. If he's critical, take it as a warning. He definitely has an idea in his head of how things should be, and he'll try to mold you into how he sees you or how he'd like to see you. Pay close attention to his naggings because, though it may seem otherwise, he means every word he says.

As a Venus-ruled sign, Taureans are true sensualists and romantic lovers. Their romantic attachments ground and stabilize them. Love is like air to them: they need it to breathe. Again, they'll want to trust and rely on you. This is essential. In fact, it's very easy to see if Taurus trusts you, at least to some degree. Taurus can't touch and make love unless he feels he can. Taurus and Virgo may be the only men in the zodiac who are mainly like this. They might entertain a fling or two in their lifetime, but that's not what they're about. Instead, they're looking for meaning and true love—someone who'll put up with their obstinate nature and even revel in it. Most of the Taurus men are quite macho. Like the bull, they're quite direct and will usually take a problem on—head on (quite the opposite of the way Cancer would handle it). Give them a good love challenge and they won't shy away. Taurus is built for competition. The problem is, he may never really stop to consider if you two are actually good for each other.

Matches with Taurus

Conventional astrological wisdom says that the lot of us is better off with those who share the same element we do or with those who feed our element (Earth with Water, for instance). This makes Taurus compatible with other Earth signs (Virgo and Capricorn) and with Water signs. Unfortunately, other Earth signs—unless they have some Air in their charts—can sometimes be too serious for Taurus, who needs a good laugh in order to let his guard down. And though Virgo is more critical of himself (and thin-skinned with others' criticisms), Taurus can sometimes take it the wrong way, too.

Quite often, Taureans are fatally attracted to Scorpios, their polar opposites. Although their elements, Earth and Water, should make them compatible, this tends to be a superficial connection. Instead, beneath the surface, they're probably at war with each other. But this just kicks up the chemistry. Taurus is also very attracted to Fire signs. This may work okay in a relationship with a Leo, but in the long run, Sagittarius and Aries may just be too big a bite to chew for more down-to-earth Taurus.

Air signs mesh well with Earth signs, too, because they're both thinking signs, whereas Water and Fire signs are more spontaneous and apt to follow their hearts more. Gemini will entertain Taurus, but Taurus won't necessarily trust her. Libra may be a good bet for Taurus, as both have an incredible affinity for an elegant, sumptuous, and refined life. Libra and Taurus manage to acquire it together by spurring each other on. Aquarius's lifestyle will drive conservative Taurus crazy, despite his attraction to her.

Virgo in Love

Virgos are inscrutable in the affairs of the heart. They seem remote and quiet one minute, then open and talkative the next. This is due only to Virgo's battle within himself. He's sensitive but doesn't like to show it. Sometimes he'll need to show you how he feels; other times, he'll keep his feelings a secret. Unfortunately, he doesn't always let you see this true side of himself. He's too busy weighing all the options and trying to act the way he thinks he should, not how he truly feels.

Virgos always need to perfect everything: every moment, every deed, and every word. They're idealists, but in a practical way. They truly believe that everything should fall into place on its own (even if it shows no sign of happening) and tend to stay in relationships much longer than they should simply because they don't want to give up and walk away. To them, you are the investment of their precious time. They also hold on to the past like Cancers and, unfortunately, apply past experiences to present ones. In a perfect world, this would make sense (to them). Unfortunately, each situation is different, and Virgos must face this fact.

Virgos try to make everything fit into their idea of a perfect world. For example, they're very serious about the words they and others use. If you tell a Virgo something, he expects you to follow through on your promise. He's put his heart and soul into finding a solution for you. If you don't at least try it his way, he'll seriously discredit you.

Matches with Virgo

Virgos are mentally attracted to Geminis, but they find the twins a bit hard to take for the long run. The light, airy nature of Geminis, too, contrasts with Virgo's obstinate nature. Gemini likes interesting discussions (as does Virgo) and entertains Virgo well, but Virgo sometimes fights more than Gemini would like.

Instead, the "grounding" present in other Earth signs may seem appealing on the surface, but leave it to a Virgo to find fault with his fellow Earth signs. Scorpios and Cancers may be the best bets, with mystical Pisces a close second. Libra sometimes goes well with Virgo but it may seem like Virgo is always just 'round the bend with Libra—never quite getting all the love and devotion he wants. Libra makes it tough.

Fire signs can be great friends with Virgo, but the two might never truly understand the other's intentions, in general. It depends on the rest of their charts. If one is true Earth, and the other is true Fire, Virgo patronizes without knowing it, and sensitive Fire signs take offense without realizing that Virgo is just trying to help. In the end, anyone with a good heart and a sensitive but practical nature will get along well with Virgo, though. Like all astrological love matches, it all depends on the partners involved.

Capricorn in Love

At times, Capricorn needs a partner who is serious, while at other times he needs a lighthearted mate who will simply make him laugh. The latter will have an almost innocent quality— a purity—that Capricorn is drawn to. Which mate Capricorn ends up with, though, depends on where he is emotionally and mentally in life. This may be true for all of us to one extent or another, but it's especially true for Capricorn.

Ultimately, Capricorn's path is always serious business. No matter how hard you make him laugh about himself and the world, his path always leads back to the same riddle. Regardless of how hard he works, how far he climbs, or how emotionally or physically rich he becomes, it's never enough. It only leads back to solitude of self.

That said, Capricorns can be very independent. They don't like being told what to do or how to do it. They seem malleable enough, and can get along with anybody, though they don't necessarily enjoy the company of all. A mate must be stimulating, engaging, knowledgeable, and, most importantly, grounded, in order for Capricorn to truly respect her. If Capricorn senses that his partner is off kilter, he'll run for the hills. He won't try to change her or help her as, say, Cancer would.

Meanwhile, if you're getting words of passion, love, and forever after, pay attention. Capricorn doesn't spew out or toss around romantic words just to woo you and then leave you cold. He's got to be somewhat convinced in order to do it. True, he's a little better at having meaningless adventures than Virgo is, but eventually he'll want something that means family and future to him. And he takes that very seriously, indeed.

Matches with Capricorn

Virgos may be too literal and spirited for Capricorn. Plus, Virgo in bed can bring out Capricorn's traditional side, which bothers Capricorn, who secretly longs for someone who can open him up, emotionally and spiritually (both in bed and out). Taurus may be too fixed, but because they both have the Earth element in common, Capricorn and Taurus can get along well.

Of all the Water signs, the intensity of Scorpios may be overwhelming—though Capricorn will get a real kick out of Scorpio's tendency to be jealous. In bed, these two can be smolderingly hot. Instead, the ambivalence of Pisces will, most likely, drive Capricorn nuts.

Strangely enough, a Leo might be the best bet for Capricorn. If Leo has some Earth in her chart—or some balanced Air—they get along well. Certainly, the attraction is there. Capricorn mystifies Leo. Capricorn praises Leo the way she needs to be praised. They complement each other, and that's what it's all about.

PART 2
TAROT

No one knows exactly when or where the Tarot originated, but the allegorical illustrations on Tarot cards are said to contain secret teachings, which in the Major Arcana represent a course in personal and spiritual development. Tarot cards are wonderful tools to use for meditation, as well as for divination. They stimulate the intuition, which is the key to the gateway of the unconscious. They illuminate the hidden factors in a person's life, factors that the person may not be aware of that are secretly shaping her existence. Thus, the Tarot is not only a tool for answering everyday questions or telling fortunes; it is also a beacon that shines light into the darkest recesses of your inner self and illuminates the vast realms that lie beyond the limits of the conscious mind.

In the view of alchemists and mystics, the symbols preserved and presented in the Tarot spring from the *anima mundi* or soul of the world, a vast repository of knowledge, like a cosmic library, filled with all the memories and wisdom of the entire human race, past, present, and future. Within this collective pool are all the basic figures found in myths, legends, religions, and fairy tales. Taken together, these figures encapsulate a magical storehouse of profound esoteric knowledge. Each figure in the Tarot calls forth from the individual's unconscious a deep resonance and, when a user consciously contacts these images in the Tarot, their hidden counterparts in the collective unconscious are allowed to surface and become integrated into the person's life. A properly conducted Tarot reading is a story. In a sense, the reading can act like a dream or a flash of inspiration to impart understanding.

CHAPTER 5

THE MAJOR ARCANA

A typical Tarot deck consists of seventy-eight cards. Of these, the first twenty-two are identified as the Major Arcana. The Major Arcana (which means mysteries or secrets) represent the mysteries or secrets of the universe that reflect universal law. As such, they are the most complex cards in the deck and require more diligence to understand. Each of the Major Arcana cards, which are also often called trump cards, is illustrated with specific symbols or scenarios, which are basically the same in all decks, even though they may differ thematically according to the philosophy of the designer. Each of the Major Arcana cards has a title, such as The Magician, The Empress, The Lovers, The Moon, The Tower, and so forth. They are numbered from zero—The Fool—to twenty-one—The World.

The cards in the Major Arcana represent forces beyond yourself and the limits of mundane, earthly, human existence. Depending on your personal worldview, you could think of these forces as fate, god, goddess, cosmic, karma, or your own higher self. Whichever way you choose to see the energies or entities behind the cards, they indicate that something larger, outside yourself is operating and influencing you and the issue about which you are seeking advice.

The Major Arcana cards possess many different layers. As you work with them, these layers reveal themselves. It's a bit like digging into an archaeological site. For example, on a strictly practical level, The Empress may be a direct reference to your mother or your desire to become a mother. On the mundane or worldly level, The Magician may refer to your desire to live a more creative life, to be more creative in your work. Each individual unfolds according to his or her own inner blueprint. There's no hurrying the process, which ultimately takes place on its own time schedule. The cycles in life show you the patterns you are following and suggest new directions. The Major Arcana can be a guide that helps us to explore universal concepts as they apply to our lives at any given moment. Let's take a look at the cards that make up this important part of the Tarot.

Note: Since its introduction in 1909, the Rider-Waite deck (which is also sometimes called the Waite deck) has been one of the most influential and popular Tarot decks. The deck was illustrated by Pamela Colman Smith, a theatrical designer, artist, writer, and member of the occult Order of the Golden Dawn. Guided by Arthur Edward Waite, Smith produced a series of seventy-eight allegorical paintings that included storytelling images on the Minor Arcana as well as the Major Arcana cards. More than 6 million Waite Tarot decks are now in print and this classic deck is widely used to illustrate books about the Tarot—including the images found next to the Major Arcana cards in this chapter—and as a teaching tool for beginning diviners.

The Fool

The Fool is a fascinating figure, yet he can be an ambiguous symbol. Related to the jester or the joker of the ordinary playing deck, which is often used as the wild card, he seems beyond ordinary cares and concerns.

Ordinarily, The Fool is shown as a person full of confidence—often the confidence of youth—and trust in the beneficence of the universe. He symbolizes that blind leap of faith that we all must take upon entering the journey of life itself, especially if that journey is spiritual.

Interpretation

When The Fool appears in a reading, depending on its position in the layout, it symbolizes someone who is about to embark on a new way of life. This may involve a physical journey, moving to a new place, starting a new job, or getting married or divorced. Often, the appearance of The Fool indicates a person who is ready to start on a spiritual path, who has made peace with the need to experience absolute faith and trust in the universe. In such a case, the person has no sense of worry or fear and feels that she is protected and that everything will turn out well. The person may be consciously in touch with the intuitive realm of his or her being, or he or she may simply be naive about what the future will bring. The Fool represents a state of openness and faith that he'll be supported in his adventure.

The Magician

The Magician is powerful, representing worldly wisdom and the control of unseen forces that operate in human lives. A deeply complex symbol, he is usually depicted as a male figure who stands alone before an array of the traditional magician's tools. In most decks, these are the symbols of the Minor Arcana suits, each of which corresponds to one of the four elements: a pentacle for Earth, a sword for Air, a cup for Water, and a wand for Fire. To possess knowledge of these elements is to gain mastery in the world. The Magician is in possession of knowledge that enables him to manipulate the material world through aligning it with the spiritual plane, in order to create the desired circumstances.

Interpretation

The appearance of The Magician in a reading indicates latent powers, yet to be taken up and brought into manifestation. Also known as The Juggler, this card suggests that everything in the universe is spread out before us, and if we learn to use them correctly we can manifest the results we desire. These are literally the basic materials of creation, and it is the task of The Magician to handle them well, to manipulate and control them for beneficent purposes. This is mental work that affects the material realm.

Thus, The Magician shows us that what we consider to be illusion is another form of reality, and what we consider to be reality can be mere illusion. This is not trickery, but a deep understanding of how we must learn to use our intellects, our intuitive abilities, our personal talents, and our practical skills in order to mediate between the two worlds, both of which affect us simultaneously.

The Magician is a card of power, for just as a mage, or true magician, stands at the center of the universe with the tools and ability to manipulate it for his purposes, so does each of us create, or re-create, our own universes within ourselves, first in our minds, and then in our manifest realities. This card tells us that our nature is one with the nature of the universe. It suggests that we have the ability to control our own lives, that we can manipulate people, things, and events—so long as we go about it the right way and for the right ends.

This card is primarily about self-development; as Tarot Arcanum One, it is the beginning of the road to spiritual enlightenment, the starting point. It does not say that we are already able to control our universes, but that we must learn what mode to use in order to gain our ends and reach our goals, whether they are spiritual or mundane.

The High Priestess

The High Priestess is a most mysterious card, representing that which has yet to be revealed, secret knowledge, the duality of life on Earth. She symbolizes feminine spiritual power, or the Goddess from whom all life comes and to whom all returns in the ever-cycling round of earthly existence.

She is depicted as a serene-faced female figure, sometimes seated with a book or scroll on her lap, which suggests the divine law that underlies the manifest universe. The scroll or book represents the Akashic Records, the divine repository of our lives past, present, and future. Sometimes, she is standing, holding a staff and pointing toward an unseen object in the distance, another indication of something yet to be revealed.

On her breast, The High Priestess wears a cross, symbolic of the four elements—Fire, Earth, Air, and Water—held in balance. She wears a crown, usually a crescent, the horns of the Moon, or a variant of it. In the Waite deck, between the horns sits a sphere, representative of the full Moon, while the horns echo the images of the waxing and waning Moon. The three lunar phases symbolize the three stages of womanhood: maiden, mother, crone.

Interpretation

When The High Priestess appears, she indicates that something hidden, or interior, is preparing to come forth or that the person needs to pay more attention to his or her inner world of dreams, imagination, and intuition. She advises you to develop awareness of the totality of yourself, the night side, so to speak, as well as the daylight personality and activities. Usually, the person is ready to accept the importance of developing this part of his or her life, but may have been holding back out of fear or inertia.

Psychologically, the underworld refers to the unconscious, or what is in the process of coming into being. In this twilight realm, of which dreams are a component, we encounter our inner selves through intuition and fantasy. The High Priestess is an image representing our potentials that have yet to be discovered and brought forth—our secret selves longing to be recognized.

The Empress

The Empress is a card of beauty and creativity, the matriarch incarnate, symbolic of the Universal Mother as monarch. She represents the social concept of the feminine in the maternal role:

procreation, nurturing, the security and comforts of home, and domestic harmony. The Empress is always a mature female figure, often seated on a throne. Full-breasted and sometimes pregnant, she symbolizes fruitfulness and earthly abundance. As a symbol of The Empress's royal position, she sometimes holds a scepter and wears an imperial crown of great magnificence. In many decks, a shield or coat of arms leans against her throne, at her feet. Many decks bear the astrological symbol for Venus, which is the planet of love, beauty, desires, and pleasure—the quintessential traditional feminine symbol.

Interpretation

When The Empress appears, a strong feminine energy is at work. As a mother figure and representative of the traditional female role, The Empress is a creative force that works for harmony. She brings disparate things together, reconciling differences, like a mother running a household must do. This is a card of emotional control and making things work congenially toward a common social goal.

The Empress also refers to the person's emotional and physical resources—for nurturing, healing, feeding, and supporting other people. Often, there is a situation in the person's life where love and nurturing are required—sometimes by the person herself, sometimes by others in the environment. This card is related to the caretaking process and may refer to the way the person was mothered, for the first and most significant relationship you form is with your mother, and this relationship has a direct bearing on all subsequent relationships. Sometimes The Empress indicates that the person either had an overbearing "smother mother," or is acting out that role.

The Emperor

The Emperor is a figure of supreme authority, as his title suggests. He is usually shown seated on a throne, sometimes flanked by animals. In the Waite deck, these are ram's heads, symbolic of masculine power. He wears robes over a full suit of armor, holds a scepter in the shape of the Egyptian ankh, and is crowned elaborately. His age and position of authority speak of experience and wisdom gained. Although he is depicted as a warrior, his attitude is one of kindness as the beneficent ruler of his empire.

The Emperor is the executive, or leader, who has reached the summit of authority and achieved worldly power. Thus, The Emperor is a father figure, as The Empress is a mother figure. He lays down the ideals, morals, and aspirations for the entire family to follow. He is the builder in the material world who strives to make constructions of lasting value and importance.

Interpretation

When The Emperor appears in a reading, look for issues related to authority. Although The Emperor represents worldly power and wisdom, he is not simply a figure who gives commands to others. His achievement is to understand that peace and security require a willingness and ability to defend it. "The price of freedom is eternal vigilance."

The Emperor is a teacher figure, and what he teaches is the meaning of power and how to use it in this world. Though not overtly aggressive, he tells us that it is necessary sometimes to take up arms against evil forces. With The Emperor, there is no waffling about what is right and good, no rationalizing that the ends justify the means. As a protective male force, especially of the home and of domestic harmony, he personifies the ideal that what is worth having is worth fighting for.

The Emperor in a reading can also indicate issues concerning one's biological father, or authority figures in general. He can show that the time has arrived to *become* the authority figure, rather than depending on others to provide protection. The Emperor often appears when the person is struggling to achieve personal independence, to overcome the inner parent tapes, to become his or her own person. The Emperor says that one must, often late in life, come to terms with what father means in his or her life, and reconcile related issues.

The Hierophant

The Hierophant is a figure with authority and power, like The Emperor, but The Hierophant's power is of a spiritual nature whereas The Emperor's is temporal. Often, he is shown as a religious leader, such as the pope of Roman Catholicism. Some decks title him The Pope. He is usually seen seated on a throne, dressed in priestly raiment, crowned, and holding a scepter. His implements will vary according to the religious theme of the deck.

His scepter symbolizes the three worlds—the physical, the astral, and the etheric. His free hand is held aloft in a position of blessing. Two or three acolytes may stand before him, either as participants, supplicants, or students, deferring to his wisdom and understanding him as a representative of religious authority. The Hierophant can be seen as a teacher to those who seek the keys to the sacred mysteries. He is responsible for making spiritual decisions for others and for blessing them. Unlike The High Priestess, whose world is primarily internal and ephemeral, The Hierophant's influence is of this world, and his spirituality can be achieved through conscious choices made on an intellectual basis.

Interpretation

The Hierophant suggests that the person has chosen a religion or philosophy with which to guide his or her life. In such a case, there is usually a great deal of loyalty to it, whatever the person's concept of God may be. Sometimes the card indicates disentangling yourself from such an association.

In some organized religions, the supreme deity does not speak to the individual directly, or to the general populace. Therefore, institutionalized religion makes use of human interpreters who convey the word of God (the divine will) to their followers.

The Hierophant symbolizes any organized institution—be it religious, philosophical, educational, spiritual, or temporal—that exerts authority over its followers or participants, a kind of mind control. In such groups, there is always a person, or a group of people, who insist that their way is the *only* way, that theirs is the ultimate truth.

Therefore, when The Hierophant appears, the idea of choice is being presented. At this stage of your spiritual development, you are challenged to remain a follower or to break out and find your own individual truth. This card suggests that you have the opportunity—and often the desire—to choose your own road to salvation, to interpret the word of God in your own way. The Hierophant asks, will you continue to depend on an outside authority, or will you learn to think for yourself? The answer is yours alone, and there may be considerable conflict concerning the issue, but what you decide will affect the rest of your life.

The Lovers

One popular image on The Lovers card shows a young couple either nude or clothed, standing apart or touching. Above them is an angel-like figure with its wings spread out over them, its hands held above their heads in a gesture of blessing. The Waite deck depicts them as Adam and Eve, standing respectively before the Tree of Eternal Life and the Tree of the Knowledge of Good and Evil. Imagery in other decks suggests choice is involved as well as the possibility of union.

Interpretation

Although many readers interpret this card as representing romantic love, it is allegorically a statement about union of opposites, whether those are a man and woman or inner conditions of conflict. The Lovers refers to discrimination in making choices. The male and female figures are symbols not only of human love and marriage but also of the dual nature within ourselves. When The Lovers card appears, it points to the need to heal an inner rift. Although it can herald a romantic involvement, it most often turns up when a critical life decision must be made, sometimes in connection with a love relationship. There are obstacles to be overcome, both within and without. This card suggests that you are at a crossroads. You have to consider all of the ramifications of the situation and choose carefully in order to further your own development and to accommodate the needs of others in the situation.

The Chariot

The Chariot is usually depicted as a strong male figure holding the reins of two Sphinx-like beasts, one black and one white. Sometimes the beasts are unicorns or other mythical creatures like Pegasus, the winged horse, or griffins. The charioteer is fully armored and carries a scepter suggesting royalty or that he is in the service of royalty. In some decks, he wears a belt and a skirt decorated with zodiacal glyphs, symbolic of time. On his shoulders are crescent moons indicating emotional factors and unconscious habit patterns that need to be changed.

The beasts pulling the chariot signify the opposing forces, which were reconciled at the stage of The Lovers and represent the person's mastery of these opposing forces and control over inner conflicts. This card suggests that before taking on outer enemies or obstacles, it is essential to be in charge of the inner opposites and stop fighting yourself. The Chariot is a symbol for the self and its direction, as is any vehicle, such as an automobile, that appears in a dream.

Interpretation

When The Chariot appears, there is a need to be in control of competing forces, whether these are inner conflicts, people, or a situation in your life that requires you to take command in order to reach your goals. Like the celebrated but seldom achieved bipartisanship of government, the solution to the problem at hand is to take the middle road between the conflicting elements.

You may feel unequal to the challenge of controlling the multiple factors of a given situation, but if you choose to just go with the flow and make the best of where it takes you, you will succeed. Once you have resolved the conflict within your own mind, even if that requires considerable struggle, you will be able to move forward. To do this, you need firm resolve—*self-mastery*. With a strategy determined by clear thinking and a sense of purpose, you will overcome all obstacles.

Receiving The Chariot in a reading, depending on its position in the spread, is generally favorable. It indicates you have the means to triumph over all obstacles and stay the course you have set for yourself. It can also mean that assistance is on the way as a result of your own strength and determination. It may suggest you are in the process of transforming yourself and your ways of thinking and behaving in order to create a firm foundation from which to go forward and achieve your desires. At this time you are keenly aware of how to use your past experience to reach a major goal and you are in touch with deep inner resources.

Strength

Most decks depict Strength as a woman in relationship to a lion. Some writers see this as a struggle, but in many decks there does not appear to be any conflict. In fact, she seems to be controlling the lion and may even seem affectionate toward him. Although many interpreters view this card as emblematic of the struggle with one's inner animal nature, others see it as symbolic of self-confidence and inner strength, of being in harmony with one's instinctive nature. The figure is taming or making friends with the powerful force represented by the animal nature. Though the lion is clearly the more physically powerful of the two, the image represents human courage and willpower that masters the instinctive realm not by force, but by cooperation.

Interpretation

When Strength appears in a reading, you are exhibiting moral courage and fortitude. You have learned to work in harmony with your own instinctive nature, to listen to it and hear its whisperings. As in tales of the hero's journey, the seeker often meets with animals, representative of the instinctive realm, who guide and help him on his way. Strength indicates that you have come through difficulties and learned to rely on inner strength to solve your problems.

This is a time when faith in yourself will pay off, when your position is strong because you have made yourself strong through suffering trials and tribulations without being defeated by them. It is a time to let people around you know who you are—especially anyone who has been dominating you.

The indication is that it is the feminine principle that does the work of reconciling the mental-rational facility with that of the intuitive-instinctive nature. The feminine is always in closer touch with nature than the masculine. Whether the reading is for a man or a woman, the same meaning applies. The lesson is that we do not conquer our animal natures by brute force (which is the typical masculine mode of approach to obstacles) but by gentleness and feeling our way into rapport with the instinctive side.

Depending on the placement of the card in the spread and the question being asked, Strength indicates that what is required in the situation is for spiritual strength to replace or overcome physical strength.

The Hermit

The Hermit is a guide figure represented as an old man, often bearded, holding a lighted lantern aloft in one hand and a staff in the other. He is usually dressed in the long robes of an anchorite or monk, plain and unadorned except for, in some decks, a knotted or tasseled cord around the waist. He radiates the wisdom of the archetypal elder figure, the sage of myth and legend. The Hermit is an ancient who is experienced on many levels and now functions as a teacher and guide. He is wise in the ways of all the worlds, visible and invisible, material and immaterial. The Hermit's solitude suggests the periodic need to withdraw from the hectic everyday world in order to regain perspective through silent reflection.

Interpretation

When The Hermit appears in a reading, it can mean that a guide figure is at hand, offering help. The querent must make an effort to connect with this guide or consciously begin a search for the truth. A second interpretation is that the questioner must voluntarily withdraw from contact with the outer world for a time in order to search his or her soul for the meaning of life. The implication is that the inner work needs to be done *now*, and that spirit cannot speak to you if you are distracted by the noise of everyday life. The answers lie in silence, and the work can only be done alone. The time has come to reunite with the Source, whether for guidance or inner balance. Sometimes, the guide figure may represent a person, such as a counselor of some sort—a therapist or clergy person—but usually it refers to inner guidance, or getting in touch with a guide from the other side.

The Wheel of Fortune

Invariably, The Wheel of Fortune card shows a wheel—often with eight spokes, a reference to the eight pagan holidays that mark the ever-turning cycles of life, death, and rebirth. The Wheel is also a symbol for the Sun's path across the sky. Human or mythical figures may also be attached to the wheel.

The Waite deck shows a sphinx holding a sword at the top of the wheel, calmly watching as the karmic wheel revolves. Around the wheel are letters that spell "Rota," a reference to the "Royal Road of the Tarot." The ascending figure on the right is a jackal-headed man, called Hermanubis, who is known for keen eyesight. A serpent descending on the left side represents the Earth and the sexual energy that arises from it. Above and below, at the four corners of the card, are winged creatures holding open books. These correspond to the bull, the lion, the eagle, and the man, symbols of the fixed signs of the zodiac, Taurus, Leo, Scorpio, and Aquarius respectively. In the Christian tradition, these refer to Matthew, Mark, Luke, and John.

Interpretation

When The Wheel of Fortune appears in a reading, it means that something has been put in motion over which you now have little or no control. You are being forced to accept the action of the forces of destiny, to get in tune with them, and to align yourself with their aims. Generally, however, the outcome is considered favorable.

These forces already set in motion foretell of changing circumstances, usually for the better, beneficial changes that will promote your growth and advancement. Balance may be an issue if you are resisting change, but you now have no choice but to go along with whatever process is working in your life. The Wheel of Fortune is a reminder that every period of intense activity must be followed by a fallow time of rest and inactivity. Where you are in your own personal cycle will be shown by the other cards in the spread.

This card almost always heralds good fortune coming as a result of what you yourself have put into motion, even if you aren't totally aware of what you have done to initiate the process. You may have applied for a new job, met a new person, begun a romance, decided to take a college course, or had a chance encounter that got the ball rolling—or the wheel turning. It means a new phase, possibly the need to make an important decision, or even a totally unexpected circumstance developing that will change your life.

Justice

The Justice card usually depicts a female figure, robed, sometimes armored, and crowned. She holds an upright sword in one hand and in the other perfectly balanced scales. In some modern decks, she is either a nude figure with arms outstretched in absolute even balance, or she is shown standing between a large set of scales while holding a smaller set. Unlike the contemporary image of Justice as blindfolded, this Justice is open-eyed, suggesting that divine justice rather than the laws of man are at work here.

Interpretation

When the Justice card appears in a reading, it can indicate that an actual legal matter is pending or being considered. Whatever the situation, you must weigh many factors in order to make a reasoned and factual assessment, i.e., judgment, of the matter at hand. The Justice card warns you to receive guidance from your inner self, not to rely solely on human advisors. Also, it cautions prudence and care, the need to deliberate calmly and carefully before taking action or concluding an outcome. Depending on what other cards appear in the spread, a third party could come to your aid and help you get the fair outcome you deserve. This card can also represent anyone involved with the legal profession—a lawyer, a judge, witnesses, law enforcement officers, and the like.

The Hanged Man

The Hanged Man is a tantalizing figure. Usually a male, hanging upside down by one leg, The Hanged Man's expression is serene, as if he is thoroughly enjoying his state. Suspended as he is by one foot, he appears to be engaged in a rather bizarre form of meditation or ritual.

In the Waite deck, The Hanged Man is shown hanging from a tree. Its roots are in the ground and the crosspiece that supports him sprouts leaves. Some authorities say this is the Tree of Life itself. Around The Hanged Man's head is a golden halo, like the rays of the Sun. Yellow is the color of Mercury, the planet of the mind. Other decks picture only the horizontal beam, but it too has leaves on it, showing that it is living wood.

Interpretation

Many writers see The Hanged Man as a card of self-sacrifice and martyrdom, but others view this tantalizing card as voluntary surrender to the process of achieving enlightenment. It may require giving up superficial pleasures and trivial activities in pursuit of a more spiritual way of life. The word sacrifice derives from the Latin *sacrāre*, which means to make sacred. Therefore, The Hanged Man may represent a sacred pursuit.

This card can indicate that a new commitment to the development of the inner self is demanded. You might need to spend time alone in order to re-evaluate just what is and what is not important to you. It may be very difficult to let go of old patterns—a relationship, a job, a worldview, a lifestyle, or a group of other people—but letting go is essential to your continued growth.

Death

The Death card tends to frighten people who see it come up in a reading, but despite its grim depiction it symbolizes the transforming powers of life, death, and rebirth. Many decks picture a skeleton with a scythe grinning toothily and wearing a black hooded robe. The Waite deck pictures Death as a man in black armor riding a white charger, suggesting the perpetual movement of the cycles of life and death.

The knight carries a banner on which is embroidered the mystical white rose, symbol of pure and true love. The rose with five petals represents the five senses of material life combined with the immortality of the heart, or soul. Greeting the knight with hands outstretched in blessing or supplication is a priest figure wearing a mitered cardinal's hat. Two children look on in awe. In the background, the Sun is rising, a sign of resurrection, over a body of water representing the unconscious realm.

Interpretation

The Death card in a reading rarely foreshadows a physical death. What it means is the end, or death, of a cycle. Whenever a stage in one's life ends, there is a need for mourning. It is only the refusal to accept that something is ending—trying desperately to hold on to what is clearly over—that causes trouble. Employing cosmetic means to stave off the approach of age, for instance, is a useless effort to avoid the inevitable. What gives importance and meaning to this card is the querent's *acceptance* of the change that cannot be avoided. Thus, in essence, the ultimate message of the Death card is the promise that new life follows disintegration.

Temperance

This lovely card often features a winged angel—male, female, or androgynous. In the Waite deck, the angel is standing in a stream bordered by flowers, with the rising Sun shining in the background. In most decks, the figure is pouring liquid—the elixir of life—from a golden vessel into a silver one in a continuous stream, suggesting the interplay of the material and spiritual worlds and the eternal flow of the waters of life. The word vessel is related to the great Mother Goddesses of antiquity, and the body is often referred to as the vessel of the soul. Thus, both the angelic figure and the cups are symbolic references to the feminine principle of cooperation, balance, harmony, receptivity, and creativity.

Interpretation

Temperance, as its name suggests, is about moderation in all things. When Temperance appears in a reading, depending on its position in the spread, you are being cautioned to have patience, which may be difficult under the circumstances. However, the circumstances of your situation will teach you to wait calmly when it seems like nothing is happening.

The person who receives Temperance in a reading is not in a position to hurry matters along. The only course is to sit and wait for things to move in their own time. The trick is to make the waiting constructive. This is one of the great lessons of the Zen masters. Learning to do nothing mindfully is a milestone on the spiritual path. It's of vital importance to know that there are times when nothing *can* be done and nothing *needs* to be done. Therein lies the state of grace.

The Devil

Many decks picture a medieval Christian-type devil, complete with horns, hooves, a hairy tail, and a pitchfork. Usually at the devil's feet are two small, humanlike figures, one male and one female, with chains around their necks that are attached to the block upon which The Devil sits. However, it is important to note that the chains are loose and the people could easily slip them off, suggesting self-imposed limitations. Whatever form The Devil takes in various decks, he is usually pretty scary looking. Occasionally, he is batlike or stylized depending on the theme of the deck and its designer's inclinations toward the figure.

The variety of illustrations implies widely differing opinions of the card's meaning. For some, the devil is a creature of consummate evil; for others the devil is a mythical creature. Many psychologically oriented people see the devil as a symbol of human indulgence, ignorance, egotism, greed, and irresponsibility. Thus, the illustration appearing on the card represents a point of view as well as the traditional meanings associated with the card.

Interpretation

Superficially, The Devil appears to be one of the more alarming cards of the Major Arcana. However, he does not represent satanic forces with evil intent, and it is important to remember this when doing readings. He is the horned god of pagan times, connected to the fertility rites banned by the Church, which feared the power of pagan rituals, especially those including sexual activity.

When The Devil shows up in a reading, depending upon his position in the spread, he is telling you that you need to re-evaluate your relationship to material things, which are keeping you chained. It's time to look at whatever is limiting you and holding you back from personal growth, especially abusive, obsessive, or harmful relationships. You are being called upon to confront your fears about financial security and social and material success—the things of this world. The Devil is a reality check that tells you to let go of old fears, hang-ups, inhibitions, and ways you manipulate others to satisfy your needs instead of taking responsibility for yourself in a positive manner. Whatever the situation, you are the only one who can change it. The two chained figures on the card represent bondage to the material realm. Their loose chains indicate your potential for attaining freedom by relinquishing obsessive ambition and excessive attachment to the things of this world.

The Tower

The Tower usually depicts a stone tower of fortress-like construction, such as those still remaining from medieval times in Europe. The Tower is in the process of falling down or being destroyed, most often by fire or lightning.

Interpretation

Like the Death card and The Devil, The Tower tends to strike alarm and fear into anyone in whose reading it appears, and indeed many writers assign a fully negative meaning to this card. The Tower does not necessarily represent ruin and devastation, although its appearance usually does herald swift and dramatic change—sometimes shocking and extremely upsetting change.

It is important to keep in mind that the querent has usually brought the situation on herself by ignoring or denying that something is rotten and needs restructuring or deconstructing. Most likely, the querent is already well aware of a pressing need to make changes, but he or she is steadfastly refusing to take action. Then along comes a circumstance, such as losing a job or getting a divorce, having an accident or a financial setback, that forces the person to face reality.

The message of The Tower is that you must destroy the old structures before they destroy you, so you can become free. Otherwise, they may be shattered by seemingly outside influences (which you have actually created yourself). In the wake of the chaos, a new order will grow. What was unsound will come tumbling down. You can pick and choose among the rubble to decide what is worth saving, and from that, rebuild your life in accordance with who you truly are.

The Star

This lovely card usually portrays a nude female figure in or beside a pool of water, pouring from two jugs, one held in each hand. In the Waite deck, she kneels and pours the contents of one pitcher into the stream and the contents of the other into the ground, showing the connection between the two feminine elements: Earth and Water. The naked woman represents unveiled truth and purity. The jugs she holds contain the waters of life. Some of the water is being returned to the Source, some is being used to infuse the land with new life.

The background of this card always displays stars; often, one directly above the figure's head is much larger than the others. Many decks show seven subsidiary stars, sometimes arranged to reflect the portal or two-pillar theme, sometimes set in a circle or a halo-like form around her. The stars sparkle above a pastoral setting—trees, mountains, birds, flowers.

Interpretation

The Star is a universal symbol of hope. Its appearance can signal the end of the travails represented by some of the earlier cards, symbolizing that a new and happier phase of life is coming into being. We see shooting stars as harbingers of good luck. From earliest times humans have been awed and fascinated by the star-spangled sky, the constellations, and the apparent motion of the bowl of the heavens.

The Star in a reading is like looking up at the bright starry sky on a clear night and seeing all the magnificence of the universe. It stimulates us to ponder the great potential of each and every human being for growth, inspiration, intuition, inner wisdom, and happiness.

Although The Star does not usually point to any specific planetary transit, as do some of the other Major Arcana cards, it does have a strong connection to astrology in general, for the zodiac signs relate to constellations. When The Star appears in a reading, it is a good time to have your horoscope read or to begin studying astrology yourself. A gate has opened for you to new possibilities. This card portends good fortune, creative inspiration, spiritual growth, help from unseen forces, and wishes come true. It marks a time of fulfillment.

The Moon

The Moon is a magical, mysterious card emblematic of the unconscious and the invisible realm of dreams, imagination, and psychic
impressions. Usually the Moon occupies the top half of the card,
sometimes shown in both its full and crescent phases with the crescent
enclosed in the full circle. In the Waite deck, drops of water fall from
the Moon, raining down on two canines, a dog and a wolf, who bay at
the Moon. Two towers, one on either side, reflect the portal theme. At
the bottom of the card is a pool or pond of water from which crawls
a crab (symbol of the astrological sign Cancer, which is ruled by the
Moon), crawfish, or lobster. The water suggests the Moon's link with
the tides, the Earth, the emotions, and the unconscious realm.

Interpretation

Astrologically, the Moon represents the soul, which is the link
between spirit (Sun) and matter (Earth). The Moon is feminine: It
symbolizes what we feel and how we respond. Therefore, it is emblematic
of all that is receptive in human nature: the subconscious, the emotions,
the instincts, and the automatic functions of the body. The lunar self is
the channel for the flow of the universal, or divine, source, and as such,
the Moon has great power. It affects everything and everyone on Earth,
from the ocean's tides to the moods and reproductive cycles of humans.

Therefore, when The Moon appears in a reading, it suggests that
you should be paying more attention to your inner/lunar self. It advises

you to illuminate your deepest nature. In its diffuse light, we can often see more clearly than in the glare of the Sun. The light of the Sun enables us to see the world around us, but the Moon allows us to illuminate what springs naturally from inside ourselves.

During the hours of night, our senses are more open and receptive to our inner spiritual harmony. When The Moon appears in a reading, it is time to attend to your dreams, feelings, instincts, and intuition.

Although traditionally The Moon card can indicate deceit and self-deception, these conditions are usually a result of ignoring your own inner promptings. If you get "taken"—especially emotionally—it's because you were letting your rational mind override your feelings. The Moon card's appearance also notifies you to take care of loose ends connected to the past, especially to your mother or other females.

The Moon is the symbol for the Goddess, whose three aspects represent the three faces of the great Triple Goddess. As the newborn crescent, the Moon is the maiden, the virgin—not chaste, but belonging to herself alone, not bound to any man. At the full Moon, she is the mature woman, sexual and maternal, giver of life. At the end of her cycle, the waning Moon about to turn dark represents the crone whose years have ripened into wisdom.

The Sun

The Sun card features a blazing Sun, sometimes with a face, with sunbeams radiating out from it. Beneath the Sun, in the Waite deck, a smiling nude child is riding a white horse. Behind him, a banner unfurls, held up by a winged staff. In the background, huge sunflowers grow against a stone wall. The Sun's planetary ruler is Leo, which is linked with children, pleasure, and creativity. The astrological Sun also rules the heart, the center of the body and the personality. The Sun card represents life itself, for the Sun gives life to everything on earth. The Sun suggests vitality, confidence, achievement, ego-attainment, and success in all endeavors.

Interpretation

When The Sun card appears, it is an indication that your past work is now bearing fruit, a concept that is symbolized by the child or children. Along with The Moon, it implies the union between the unconscious realm of creativity (Moon) and the conscious realm of manifestation (Sun). Whether the birth represented is a biological child or a creative project, the outcome is a happy one. It is a time when good things come into your life—success, optimism, achievement, health, general good fortune, and happiness.

When The Sun turns up, it brightens any negative cards in the spread—no matter where The Sun appears in the spread. His influence is always beneficial, suggesting prosperity, enthusiasm, honors, public recognition, and attainment. You are happy to be alive because you feel it is the dawning of a new day. Any special efforts or ventures, such as taking a test or making a presentation, will turn out favorably.

In the wake of the demise of the great Mother Goddess as the sole divinity, the Sun, which represents the masculine principle, came to be worshipped as the central deity in many cultures. The ancient Egyptians, after eons of a pantheon of goddesses and gods, under the leadership of the pharaoh Akhenaten, were persuaded, albeit reluctantly, to accept a single god—known as Ra, Amun-Ra, or Aten (all of which were names for the Sun)—which Akhenaten believed was the god of all gods. The Greeks called their Sun god Helios, whom the Romans named Apollo.

Judgment

The Judgment card visually seems rather negative. In the Waite deck, a winged figure, whom some call the angel Gabriel, emerges from a cloud and blows a trumpet. Beneath him are several nude figures of men and women looking up, hearing the trumpet's blast. Their arms are outstretched, and they seem to have risen from coffins or the earth itself. Their expressions reveal awe tinged with fear.

Of all the allegorical symbolism of the Major Arcana, this is the most purely Christian, suggesting the feared Day of Judgment, when God will judge all souls and apportion out rewards or punishments accordingly. However, this is not a totally Christian idea; the Egyptians and other cultures also expressed the notion of the soul being judged. The goddess Maat, for instance, weighs the soul against her Feather of Truth. Whether seen from a Christian point of view (which these medieval images represent) or from a universal one, the idea behind the symbols is that of an awakening.

Interpretation

When the Judgment card appears, what is being awakened is a sense of a higher self within. Sometimes the card coincides with a person turning away from a traditional set of beliefs toward one that better suits his or her personal philosophy of life. Judgment represents the end of something—an old way of life, a cycle that is finished. It is a time to seek new direction, to make adjustments that reflect who your truly are—perhaps by breaking away from your conventional way of life and believing.

Generally speaking, this is a positive card symbolizing regeneration and rebirth into wholeness after a period of confusion and a sense of confinement (shown by the coffins). You may have been feeling "dead" in your old life. When Judgment appears, you have the unique opportunity to relive, to enliven yourself and your environment by making the appropriate changes. What is ending is doubt and indecision, depression and despair, fear and inhibition. It's a time of new freedom to be yourself.

The World

In many decks, The World card shows a young woman, sometimes nude or wearing a long scarf. The scarf covers her genitals but leaves her breasts bare. In each hand, she holds a double-ended wand that points both upward and downward, suggesting, "As above, so below." In the Waite deck, she is surrounded by an oval-shaped wreath.

As with The Wheel of Fortune card, to which The World is related, the four corners of the card feature a bull, a lion, an eagle, and a man—representing the four fixed signs of the zodiac: Taurus, Leo, Scorpio, and Aquarius. These elemental figures also depict the four directions.

Interpretation

This is the last numbered card of the Major Arcana. It represents balance and support by unseen forces and symbolizes the end of the spiritual journey begun by The Fool. To embark upon the spiritual journey is to invite unseen forces to interact with us. These creative energies manifest in many ways, and often serve as guides. Guides bring us into grace and show the way. To encounter a guide—and they come in many guises—is to enter another realm, a place of great powers and, sometimes, great secrets. This realm belongs to the invisible world, although its denizens can, like angels, assume human or animal form. To interface with this world is to be impacted in a way that is life-changing. With guides, we enter a world of supreme power—not the power of the material world but of the invisible order that supports and nourishes our world and our lives here. It is the realm of the sacred.

When The World card appears in a reading, it is a signal that you have been guided to the successful conclusion of your spiritual journey. At this, the final stage, you will receive what is rightfully yours because you have earned it. Now you are and feel whole, complete. You are refreshed from your long journey and ready to begin anew at a higher level.

CHAPTER 6

THE MINOR ARCANA

Most scholars agree that the Minor Arcana were added to the Major Arcana sometime in the fourteenth or fifteenth century. It is believed that this portion of the Tarot was originally used for fortune-telling, and that in earlier times, it was considered safe for nonadepts to have access to this part of the Tarot. The Minor Arcana consists of four suits of fourteen cards each: Wands, Pentacles, Swords, and Cups. In medieval times the four suits represented the four main classes of people—the nobility, the clergy, the merchant class, and the working class. In today's society, there are correspondences—an elite, or old money, class is the nobility; today's version of the clergy has expanded to include the professions and academia; the merchant class includes businesses and people employed by corporate institutions; and those in blue-collar or service positions are the working class. These suits help us pinpoint the areas of life that need our attention, because each of the suits represents a distinct realm of activity, experience, and personal growth. When many cards of the same suit appear in a reading, it's a clear indication that the person consulting the Tarot is concerned about a particular area of life—or should be.

Each suit contains four Court cards (King, Queen, Knight, and Page) and ten number cards from Ace through Ten, also called pip cards.

- **King:** A king is a powerful ruler who exercises absolute authority over the territory he rules. Thus, the King of any suit represents a completion point: There's no higher position to attain.

The level of the King is where you release and let go, complete old tasks, and prepare for a new and more fulfilling way of life.

- **Queen:** The Queen may portray a mature, capable woman, an authority figure who is nurturing and understanding, or a mother image, sometimes the querent's real mother. With the Queen, you achieve a level of maturity and self-confidence.

- **Knight:** At the level of the Knight, you are fully aware of your path, and your aims are clear. You feel an intense sense of dedication—to a project, an idea, a person. You've taken risks and gotten yourself together for the task at hand, and you are focusing your energies totally toward accomplishing your goal, in order to make the risk worthwhile.

- **Page:** The Page represents preparing yourself in order to succeed at something. It involves being willing to assume a subordinate role—as younger people often are—and to learn about commitment. The Page is about challenging yourself, developing your inner resources, and taking something to a greater stage of accomplishment. You may experience some hesitancy, or feel that you are not fully prepared for the task, but you still hope the situation will turn out as you anticipate.

- **The Numbered Cards:** Each suit also includes an Ace, which is considered to be the One card, followed by cards numbered Two through Ten. Also known as pip cards, these combine the qualities of the suit with those of the number. In many decks, the pip cards do not display *any* scenarios to suggest the card's meaning, but merely show the corresponding number of the suit symbol. For example, the Three of Cups may simply depict three cups, without any storytelling imagery.

Generally speaking, the cards of the Minor Arcana represent lesser, or mundane, lessons. They show the everyday concerns, situations, challenges, and achievements you experience in your personal life. As such, they also present advice and describe conditions and possibilities related to the subject of a reading. When many (or all) of the cards in a reading come from the Minor Arcana, it's safe to say your future is in your own hands. Your decisions and actions will produce your future. You have the ability to control your destiny.

Let's take a look at the various suits and how their cards can help you divine your future.

The Suit of Wands

The suit of Wands corresponds to the element of Fire. Fire is active, outer-directed, linked with spirit, will, self-expression, and inspiration. It suggests growth, expansion, and personal power. Because Fire represents archetypal masculine or yang energy, the symbolism used to depict this suit in the Tarot is distinctly phallic. Some decks use other images for the suit of Wands—rods, staves, clubs, branches sprouting leaves, lances, arrows, torches, or divining rods.

Often the people on the Wands cards are shown as warriors, heroes, leaders, or magicians, dynamic and creative people who charge forth into life with confidence and enthusiasm. They may ride proud steeds, wave flags, or wear garlands. Whatever they are doing, they seem to be enjoying themselves.

When Wands appear in a spread or reading, it's usually an indication that some sort of action or growth is afoot. You might be embarking on an adventure of some kind or may be required to muster your courage in a challenging endeavor. Perhaps you could benefit from using your intuition instead of logic to solve a problem. Maybe you need to have fun, take some risks, assert yourself, or be creative.

King of Wands

The King of Wands is usually shown as a dignified man, seated on a throne, robed and crowned. Sometimes he wears armor; other times he appears as a prosperous merchant king. A positive and powerful figure, he is clearly in command of the situation, confident and at ease. He holds a full-length staff or rod, generally upright but sometimes leaning against his shoulder. In some decks, this King faces sideways, and whether he is looking toward or away from other cards in a spread will have a bearing on his relationship to the reading.

Queen of Wands

The Queen of Wands is pictured as a statuesque woman of regal bearing. She holds a tall staff in one hand, a symbol of her authority. Often she sits on a throne, robed and crowned, but some decks show her as a well-dressed matron figure.

Knight of Wands

The Knight of Wands is usually depicted as a young man on a rearing horse, in a mode of forward action. He is brandishing the wand like a weapon, but it seems more for show than to render a blow. He usually wears a suit of armor that is colorful and ornate. His position indicates that he is riding toward some encounter, more likely a joust than a fight.

Page of Wands

The Page of Wands shows a youth, generally facing sideways and holding a tall staff before him with both hands, perhaps leaning on it. His attitude is expectant but casual. He is wearing garb similar to that of the rest of the royal court, but because he is a youth he may wear short pants. Some contemporary decks depict the Page as a girl or an androgynous figure.

The Suit of Pentacles

Pentacles or pentagrams (five-pointed stars) correspond to the Earth element. Like Water, Earth is a feminine/yin force that energetically relates to our planet as the source of sustenance, security, and stability. The suit of Pentacles represents practical matters, money and resources, the body, and the material world. Tarot decks often portray the suit as coins or disks, sometimes as shields, stones, rings, shells, crystals, wheels, stars, clocks, or loaves of bread. Regardless of the actual image used, the suit symbolizes physical resources, values, practical concerns, material goods, property, and forms of monetary exchange—things that sustain us on the earthly plane.

Storytelling decks often depict people on the Pentacles cards engaged in some form of work or commerce, or enjoying the fruit of their labors and the things money can buy. The Three of Pentacles in the Waite deck, for instance, shows a craftsman working at a forge. The Ten of Pentacles presents a picture of domestic security, abundance, and comfort. The Five of Pentacles, on the other hand, portrays a sad image of poverty and need.

When Pentacles appear in a spread, it's a sign that financial or work-related matters are prominent in the mind of the person for whom the reading is being done. In some cases, these cards can also signify physical or health issues, or other situations involving the body or one's physical capabilities. The Queen of Pentacles, for example, can indicate a sensual woman who is at home in her body, who loves good food, creature comforts, and the finer things in life. Depending on the cards, this suit may suggest a need to focus on practical concerns. Or you could be too security-conscious and are putting emphasis on material things at the expense of spiritual, emotional, or intellectual considerations.

King of Pentacles

The King of Pentacles is usually shown as a royal figure regally dressed and seated on a throne. In some decks, the throne is decorated with animal figures such as a lion, a bull, an eagle, or a griffin (signifying the four fixed signs of the zodiac). He may or may not be crowned, but he appears comfortable with the power money confers. Generally the King holds a single coin upright in one hand and a scepter in the other, and he is sometimes represented as a prosperous merchant.

Queen of Pentacles

The Queen of Pentacles is a benevolent figure with a regal and kindly bearing, sometimes shown holding the pentacle or coin in her lap and gazing fondly down at it. She may also be pictured standing, leaning against an ornate throne or chair. Like the King, her throne is often decorated with animal figures. She is someone who understands and respects money as a tool, but does not worship it.

Knight of Pentacles

This Knight brings news concerning money, usually good news. He is typically depicted on horseback, facing sideways, wearing armor, and holding the pentacle before him as if offering it to someone. Unlike the Knight of Wands who is on a charging horse, the Knight of Pentacles' horse is at parade rest, calm and stable. He is poised on the edge of adventure or travel.

Page of Pentacles

The Page of Pentacles is often shown as a youth standing in a meadow or countryside. He is holding the pentacle before him, as if admiring it. His attitude suggests that he desires money or wants to achieve the means to gain it, perhaps through education or apprenticeship. Sometimes called the card of the student or scholar, the Page of Pentacles shows one who is so intent on his lessons that he misses everything else that's going on around him. In some contemporary decks, the Page is pictured as a girl or androgynous figure.

The Suit of Swords

The suit of Swords relates to the element of Air. Like Fire, Air is a masculine/yang force, so its symbol, too, is obviously phallic. Although usually depicted as a mighty battle sword, the suit's symbol may be represented by ordinary knives, athames (ritual daggers used by magicians), scythes, axes, guns, or spears. Some swords are sturdy and functional, others are ornate, reminiscent of King Arthur's Excalibur. In The Wheel of Change deck, Swords are presented as shards of broken glass. However, the "weapon" represented by this suit is the intellect. As such, Swords symbolize rational thinking, logic, analysis, communication, and the power of the mind.

When Swords turn up in a reading, it often means that mental or verbal activity is a priority. Perhaps you are overworking your mind. Or you might need to use your head and examine an issue clearly and rationally. The King of Swords, for instance, can advise you not to let your heart rule your head. Swords also represent communication, study, or cutting through murky situations with logic and discrimination.

King of Swords
The King of Swords is a somewhat stern figure who is in absolute command, but who can be trusted to be fair in his judgment and decisions. He is usually pictured enthroned, armored, helmeted, and crowned, a combination of symbols that suggests not only power and authority, but a willingness to use it forcefully if necessary. In one deck, he holds a set of balanced scales suggesting both justice and the sign of Libra. Some Tarot experts attest that his sign is Gemini. Regardless of which zodiacal sign he refers to, the suit of Swords corresponds to the element of Air. Therefore, his appearance often has to do with your mental processes.

Queen of Swords
The Queen of Swords is the female counterpart of the King, except that she represents the emotional and creative side of the

mental processes. A mature woman who sits on an ornate throne and wears beautiful robes, she holds her sword in one hand and reaches out with the other in a gesture suggesting permission to rise and come forward. She is a formidable figure with power and authority, either in the mental world or in the spiritual realm.

Knight of Swords

The Knight of Swords is often shown leaning forward on a fully charging horse, his sword held upright and forward as if he is ready to encounter the enemy. He is definitely on the attack and by his expression he expects to win the battle. He can represent a person who is overly aggressive or argumentative, who lives in attack mode. Or he can mean that you are aggressively pursuing a lifestyle that will allow you to live out your own philosophical ideals.

Page of Swords

The Page of Swords is about risk on a mental or spiritual level. It might mean you are taking up some new line of thought or study. Many decks depict a youth standing, looking over his shoulder away from the sword he holds. He seems a bit unsure of his ability to wield the weapon although he tries to appear as if he can easily defeat any enemy. He usually wears a short garment, leather or padded cloth, instead of armor. Some contemporary decks show the Page as a girl or androgynous figure.

The Suit of Cups

The suit of Cups is associated with the element of Water. Water's energy is receptive, inner-directed, reflective, connected with the emotions, creativity, and intuition. Because Water is a feminine or yin element, its symbols suggest the womb. In the Tarot, Cups are usually shown as chalices or goblets, but any type of vessel can depict the nature of the suit. Some decks picture them as bowls, cauldrons, vases, urns, flowers, pitchers, coffee mugs, steins, baskets, or bottles. Regardless of the imagery, the principle is the same—Cups represent the ability to receive and hold.

For the most part, the scenes that appear on these cards suggest comfort, security, and contentment. Because the suit of Cups represents the emotions, the people on the cards are usually shown in relationships of some kind—romantic, familial, friendship. The Two of Cups symbolizes partnership, and frequently a man and woman appear together in a loving manner on the card. Three women friends often grace the Three of Cups, while the Ten of Cups depicts a happy home and family life.

A reading that contains many Cups usually emphasizes emotions and/or relationships. Depending on the cards involved, you may be enjoying positive interactions with people you care about or are seeking greater fulfillment in matters of the heart. Perhaps you are suffering a loss or disappointment, or are on your way to recovery and emotional renewal.

King of Cups

The King of Cups has a loving demeanor. He is a mature man, usually pictured seated on a throne, often with water in the background. In the Waite deck, his crown is more like an elaborate hat than a bejeweled regal headpiece, suggesting that he stands with rather than above his subjects. Rarely is he shown wearing armor—usually plain robes—so there is nothing of the militant about him. This King's expression is benign, his attitude relaxed and nonthreatening.

Queen of Cups

The Queen of Cups is a beautiful and benevolent figure. The cup she holds is an ornate chalice, and she gazes at it as if she could see visions of the future inside. She wears robes that appear to be filmy and flowing, and her crown is elaborate but graceful. Usually she is pictured with water flowing at her feet, for this suit corresponds to the Water element. An affectionate and loving woman, whether wife, mother, friend, or lover, she is wise in the ways of the human heart. Her attitude is one of receptiveness and approachability.

Knight of Cups

Portrayed as a handsome young man, usually sitting upright on a white horse in parade or dressage position, he holds the cup straight out in front of him. His helmet may be winged, a symbol of the messenger. In this case, the message he brings is of love or good tidings. Usually depicted in an outdoor setting, sometimes with water under the horse's hooves, this Knight is armored only lightly. He's a lover, not a fighter.

Page of Cups

The Page of Cups usually shows a young man in decorative short garb wearing an elaborate hat. His attitude is relaxed and open, and he seems well pleased with himself. In the Waite deck, he holds the cup out in one hand—a fish, symbol of the Water element, peeks out of it. It's as though he magically produced the fish like a rabbit out of a hat, and he seems to expect approval. Some decks depict the Page as a girl or androgynous figure.

CHAPTER 7

INTERPRETING THE TAROT

The first step in learning to interpret the Tarot is to familiarize yourself with your own deck of cards. The images on the cards resonate differently with different people and your interpretation will depend upon your individual temperament as well as on your purpose for using the Tarot. Your own first impressions of the cards may differ from the interpretations you read here, or in any other book. This does not mean you are wrong; this book is only a guideline. Each person's reaction to the cards is as unique as a fingerprint. The rule of thumb is to do what makes sense to you.

In this chapter, you'll learn how to interpret your cards, information on the symbolism in the deck, and how to use your own intuition to figure out what the cards are trying to tell you.

One Step at a Time

When you first begin serious study of the Tarot, you may wish to spend the first hour of every day working with the cards. You can also learn the symbols and their meanings bit by bit as you practice laying out cards and interpreting them.

If you do not have the leisure to spend the first hour of the day with your cards, at least set aside some specific time, preferably daily, or as often as you can manage.

1. **Step One:** Begin by concentrating on each of the Major Arcana cards in turn. Begin with Trump zero, The Fool.

2. **Step Two:** After you have familiarized yourself with the Major Arcana—the heart of the Tarot—turn to the Minor Arcana. Study the meanings of the four suits, for each suit corresponds to an area of life and represents a mode of interacting with the world.

3. **Step Three:** Next, move on to the Court cards: the Kings, Queens, Knights, and Pages. These cards often are used to represent people, although they have other meanings and purposes, too. Become familiar with the images on these cards and the distinctions between them.

4. **Step Four:** Last, examine the numbered cards of the Minor Arcana. When you have become familiar with all seventy-eight cards, you can begin to practice readings.

At first the task of remembering all seventy-eight cards may seem a bit overwhelming. But little by little, you'll find yourself growing more comfortable with the images, and you'll start to grasp the inherent system at work within the two books of the Tarot. Your intuitive responses will begin to make sense. You'll start to see connections between the cards that turn up in your daily sessions and what's going on in your life. Before long, you will find yourself gaining an appreciation of the breadth and depth of this time-honored source of wisdom that has fascinated some of the world's greatest minds for centuries.

Trust Your Intuition

As you familiarize yourself with your personal tarot deck, remember, when you use the Tarot you are tapping your intuition, and intuition is not logical or rational. If you tend to be predominantly left-brained (as most of us are), this might at first seem a bit strange. You may experience odd sensations, such as a mild pulsing in the forehead, a tingling, lightness, or an impression of being pulled inward. Do not let this frighten you. Your intuition cannot hurt you; it's a natural part of you, just like your other senses.

Your intuition, or sixth sense, is a valuable and often underutilized resource. In your unconscious, you have a huge data bank of experiences upon which to draw, most of which you are not even aware of. As a result, you really know much more than you think you know. Your intuition has the unique ability to access knowledge and to correctly interpret the cards *for you*. In short, your unconscious is an innovator with great creative ability. Pay attention to it, trust it, let it guide you in your study of the Tarot—and in life.

However, if at any time you feel uncomfortable while using the cards, stop and try again later. Pay attention to negative feelings. Make notes about any cards or symbols that produce anxiety or discomfort. Negative information is only that—*information*. Psychic information is like a weather forecast: If we know the weather is going to be stormy, we can take sensible precautions.

Symbolism in the Cards

Every detail on each card—especially those in the Major Arcana (Chapter 5)—is a meaningful symbol. Symbols resonate on different levels of the psyche. One of the best ways to connect with these symbols is to contemplate and meditate upon those that are meaningful to *you*. The symbols produced by your unconscious mind are truly yours. Thus, there are as many interpretations of the symbols of the Tarot cards as there are readers. How a card speaks to you and how you feel about the symbols it presents is what's important.

Color Symbolism

Many Tarot decks display vivid and beautiful color palettes. But the colors shown on the cards are not purely decorative; they embody specific symbolic, spiritual, psychological, and physiological properties as well. For centuries, artists have used colors in their compositions, not only for their aesthetic properties, but also for their ability to convey moods and messages to those who view them.

In magical practice, colors correspond to the four elements. Red is associated with Fire, blue with Water, green with Earth, and yellow with Air. Because each suit is linked with an element, many Tarot artists use the colors connected with the corresponding suits to trigger subconscious responses and insights. Therefore, some decks emphasize red on the cards in the suit of Wands, blue on the Cups cards, green on the Pentacles cards, and yellow on the Swords cards.

Studies show that people react psychologically and even physically to colors. For instance, red tends to make us feel stimulated, warmer, and can even raise pulse rate and body temperature slightly. Blue, conversely, calms and cools us. In some prisons, cell walls were painted pink and aggressive behavior among inmates declined. The table below lists qualities associated with different hues. As you familiarize yourself with your Tarot deck, notice how the artist has used colors to express certain qualities.

Color	Intention
Red	Passion, vitality, courage
Orange	Warmth, energy, activity, drive, confidence
Yellow	Creativity, optimism, enthusiasm
Green	Healing, growth, fertility, prosperity
Light blue	Purity, serenity, mental clarity, compassion
Royal blue	Loyalty, insight, inspiration, independence
Indigo	Intuition, focus, stability
Purple	Wisdom, spirituality, power
White	Purity, wholeness, protection
Black	Power, the unconscious, banishing, wisdom
Pink	Love, friendship, affection, joy, self-esteem
Brown	Grounding, permanence, practicality

Popular Symbols

In addition to the suit symbols, you'll find many familiar—and some not so familiar—images on the cards in your deck. Tarot artists intentionally choose symbols from various spiritual, cultural, magical, and psychological traditions to convey information directly to your subconscious. Like dream imagery, the symbols depicted on Tarot cards speak to people at a deep level and trigger insights in a way that's more immediate and succinct than words can.

Symbols and pictures offer other advantages over words, too. Because images are understood by our inner knowing, they are less likely to present you with dogma when you seek truth. They inspire you to think, but they don't tell you what to think. They bypass the analytical, orderly left brain and strike up a lively conversation with the imaginative, flexible right brain. Like myths, symbols transcend the boundaries of religion, nationality, and time, presenting universal themes and concepts that people everywhere can relate to.

The cards in the Major Arcana, in particular, are rich with meaningful imagery, although many decks include vivid symbolism on the Minor Arcana cards as well. Some of the symbols are universal in nature, found in many countries and time periods. Others are personal and may reflect the designer's intentions or beliefs, rather than holding broader meanings for all users. The Universal Tarot, by Maxwell Miller, incorporates a variety of symbolism from many different traditions to create a complex and comprehensive oracle.

Universal Symbolism

Symbols embody the essence of whatever they stand for; they aren't merely a convenient form of shorthand. That's why they have such power, why they appear in diverse and widely separated cultures, and why they have endured for millennia.

Symbols that turn up again and again, in all parts of the world, possess universal appeal and resonate in what Swiss psychiatrist C.G. Jung called the collective unconscious. They mean essentially the same thing to everyone, regardless of age, race, religion, or nationality and get around the limitations of the rational, analytical left brain. Often we confront these symbols in dreams where they provide guidance and awaken us to parts of ourselves that we may have ignored in our waking lives. The Tarot works in a similar manner.

The following table shows a number of common, universally understood symbols that you may notice on the cards in your Tarot deck. They can be helpful keys as you examine the cards and learn their significances.

Symbol	Meaning
Circle	Wholeness, unity, protection, continuity
Square	Stability, equality, structure
Triangle	Trinity, three-dimensional existence, movement
Downward triangle	Divine feminine, Earth or Water elements
Upward triangle	Divine masculine, Fire or Air elements
Star	Hope, promise
Five-pointed star	Protection, the human body, physical incarnation
Six-pointed star	Union of male/female or Earth/sky, integration, manifestation
Vertical line	Movement, heaven, sky, masculine energy
Horizontal line	Stability, Earth, feminine energy
Cross	Union of male/female or Earth/sky, integration, manifestation
Spiral	Life energy, renewal, movement toward the center

Sun	Clarity, vitality, optimism, contentment, masculine energy
Moon	Secrets, intuition, emotions, feminine energy
Dove	Peace, reconciliation, promise
Crane	Wisdom
Rose	Love
Mountain	Challenge, vision, achievement
Ocean/water	Emotions, the unknown depths of the psyche
Snake	Transformation, hidden knowledge, kundalini energy
Egg	Birth, fertility
Rainbow	Renewal, hope, happiness
Book	Knowledge
Lantern	Guidance, clarity, hope
Bridge	Connection, harmony, overcoming difficulty
Tree	Knowledge, growth, protection, strength
Butterfly	Transformation

When studying the symbolism in the Tarot, remember that your own responses and interpretations are what count most. Cars suggest movement and freedom to most people, but if you were in a serious auto accident when you were young, cars may represent pain or danger to you. Trust your own instincts and intuition. After all, your Tarot deck and your subconscious are attempting to communicate with you, and they will do it in imagery that you can understand.

CHAPTER 8

TAROT SPREADS

After you've learned the meanings of the individual cards and the symbolism inherent in them, you can begin to combine them into significant patterns or spreads. Spreads are configurations of Tarot cards that have been designed to convey information in a particular way. The simplest spreads use only a single card; complex patterns may involve more than a dozen. A reading can include one or several spreads, depending on the situation and what you want to know. The spreads here offer a variety of approaches. You should experiment with all of them to see which ones work best for you.

Acquainting Yourself with Spreads

Spreads are configurations or arrangements of cards—usually three or more, and up to more than a dozen—designed to convey when all the pieces are in place. In a spread, each position within the overall pattern means something specific. The relationships between the cards become as important as the individual cards themselves. Some spreads form designs that represent significant spiritual symbols. Other spreads are more open-ended and can be adapted to address a variety of possibilities. The cards in a three-card spread, for instance, may be viewed as signifying one of the following.

- The past, present, and future
- The physical, mental, and spiritual aspects of a question
- The situation, recommended action, and likely outcome

You'll probably find that some spreads appeal to you more than others or are more useful for your purposes. None is better than another; the choice of which spread(s) to use is yours entirely. After you become experienced at working with the Tarot, you might decide to design your own spreads or adapt traditional spreads to suit yourself, but before you do that, let's take a look at some techniques and some of the more commonly used spreads.

Choosing a Significator

One of the first steps in laying out many spreads is to choose a Significator, a card the querent selects to represent herself in a reading. This card usually is incorporated into the spread, although sometimes it is laid aside face up where it symbolizes the person for whom the reading is being done. In some cases, a Significator could represent a group or organization, a situation or event.

Choose a card that best describes the person or matter about which you are inquiring. You can either remove the Significator card from the pack or leave it in, according to the layout you are using. For instance, the Celtic Cross spread begins by the querent consciously picking a Significator, removing it from the deck, and placing it as the first card in the spread. Here, the Significator serves as the center, or grounding point, of the layout. If the Significator is left in the deck and it turns up in the spread, the position it occupies becomes particularly important.

If you like, you can use only the Major Arcana cards in a spread. In this case, your Significator will also be a trump card, and it plays a key role in your reading.

Laying Out a Spread

If a Significator is called for, select it from the deck. Then choose a spread you feel is suitable to the question or issue at hand and lay out the cards according to the instructions in this chapter. Different spreads are designed to answer different sorts of questions or to comment on certain types of situations. If you don't know which spread is best for your question, you can use the Celtic Cross spread, shown in this chapter. This versatile pattern was recommended by Arthur Edward Waite as "the most suitable for obtaining an answer to a definite question."

Next, proceed with whatever shuffling method you have decided to use. Many readers encourage the querent to shuffle the cards, in order to put his or her vibrations on them. Other readers prefer not to let anyone else touch their cards. The choice is up to you. No matter how you shuffle, or who shuffles, the cards will automatically arrange themselves as they should be. Count on it! The order in which they come up is never an accident.

The querent (you or someone else) then cuts the cards. After cutting and reassembling the deck, begin dealing the spread from the top of the deck. Some readers lay the cards face down; others, face up. Again, the choice is yours. Regardless of whether the querent sits across from or beside the reader, the cards are always read as they face the reader. If you deal cards face down, be sure to turn them up from left to right so that you don't reverse upright cards or turn reversed cards upright.

Some writers on Tarot insist that the rest of the deck be kept face down at all times. Once a layout is dealt, the remaining cards may be laid aside and left out of the reading. Or if you prefer, hold the unused part of the deck as you read and, when it seems appropriate, for elucidation or to answer further questions regarding the matter, draw cards at random from the deck. As you continue doing readings, you will develop your own methods. There is no right way.

Common Spreads

There are many common spreads that you can use to divine the future and read the Tarot. Here are some of the most common.

Single-Card Method

This is the easiest and most basic of all spreads, and it can be used to answer all types of questions. Although you won't get as much in-depth information as you would from a longer, more complex spread, this method can be surprisingly helpful—especially in answering straightforward questions for which you need an immediate answer.

Shuffle and cut the cards while thinking about your question. Then draw a single card from the pack. You can either pick the top card from the deck or fan out all the cards face down and select one at random. The card's meaning will shed light on your question.

Yes/No Method

To use the Yes/No method, you need only decide which cards will represent yes and which no. After the usual shuffling and cutting, draw a single card from the deck, either from the top or at random. Consider the card's meaning, too, for this will provide further information. There are no firm rules, but here are some guidelines:

Designating Yes/No Cards

Major Arcana	
If you are willing to work with the concept of the card.	Yes
If you are unwilling to do the work.	No
Minor Arcana	
Even Numbers	Yes
Odd Numbers	No
Court Cards	
King	No
Queen	Yes
Knight	No
Page	Yes

Once you have decided which cards mean yes and which indicate no, you should also consider whether your chosen card is upright or reversed.

- **Upright:** If it's a Yes card, the upright position represents a definite Yes. If it's a No card, the upright position indicates a definite No.
- **Reversed:** If Yes, there will be a delay. If No, there will be obstacles to prevent you.

You may use these guidelines or you may opt to create a system of your own for determining which cards signify yes and which ones signify no for you.

Either/Or Method

Use this spread when you have two options and can't decide between them. After shuffling and cutting the deck, select two cards either from the top or at random from the pack. The first card represents one option, the second card signifies the other choice.

Past-Present-Future Method

This three-card spread lets you see the past influences or conditions regarding a situation, the present state of the matter, and what's likely to occur in the future. After shuffling and cutting the deck, select three cards either from the top of the pack or at random. Lay them out side by side. The card on the left represents the past; the middle card shows the present; the card on the right indicates the future.

Immediate Situation Three-Card Spread

This simple, quick layout focuses on what's happening now and provides insight into the matter at hand. It's a good spread to use when you want to focus on a particular situation, clarify what's happening, and receive insight or a new perspective.

Card 1: The nature of the present situation
Card 2: Your attitude toward what's happening
Card 3: The key element for you to consider

Four-Card Spread

This spread offers advice for dealing with a specific concern. Its strength is its simple, direct approach to dealing with practical, everyday problems. Shuffle and cut the cards, then lay them out side by side in a horizontal line, from left to right.

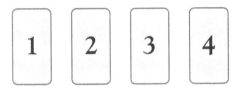

Card 1: Situation
Card 2: Obstacle
Card 3: Action recommended
Card 4: Outcome

Traditional Celtic Cross Spread

This popular and versatile spread calls for a Significator. Place it on the table to bring you (or the person for whom the reading is being done) into the reading and lay Card 1 on top of the Significator.

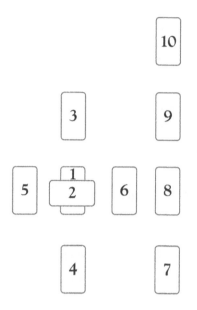

Card 1: This covers you and describes your immediate concerns.

Card 2: This crosses you and describes obstacles facing you.

Card 3: This crowns you and describes what is known to you objectively.

Card 4: This is beneath you and describes the foundation of the concern or past influences affecting the situation. It can also show what is unknown about the situation.

Card 5: This is behind you and describes past influences now fading away.

Card 6: This is before you and describes new circumstances coming into being—the near future.

Card 7: This is your self and describes your current state of mind.

Card 8: This is your house and describes the circumstances surrounding the situation.

Card 9: This is what you hope or fear, perhaps both what you what you want *and* fear.

Card 10: This is what will come and describes the likely future outcome.

Interpreting a Spread

It's important to look at any spread first as a whole. Before you start interpreting the individual cards and their placements, look at the overall picture. What colors are most evident? Are the images powerful and dramatic or peaceful and benign? Is the general tone one of contrasts or of harmony? How do you feel when you gaze at the spread?

Next, check for similarities, voids, preponderances, or weaknesses. Does the spread contain many Major Arcana cards or mostly Minor Arcana ones? Are Court cards present? Aces? Are there many cards from the same suit? Is any suit absent? Do several of the numbered cards bear the same number?

Timelines and Levels of Awareness

If the spread indicates a timeline, as is the case with the Past-Present-Future spread and the Celtic Cross, notice which cards appear in the beginning and at the end of the time period represented. If the "past" includes negative cards and the "future" shows positive ones, you can see definite progress being made and better days ahead. If the opposite is evident, it could indicate that you aren't handling the situation appropriately or that things may get worse before they get better.

Numbers in Spreads

Pay attention to the numbers shown on the pip cards and where they fall in the spread. Do you see lots of Fours and Eights, indicating stability, or Fives suggesting change? In a time-oriented spread, do low numbers turn up early in the spread and higher numbers later on? This can show development with regard to the subject of the reading. Consider the numbers on the trump cards as well as those on the Minor Arcana cards.

After you've assessed the spread from a broad perspective, you can zero in on the meanings of the individual cards in their respective positions. By combining the meanings of each card with its position, you can gain highly personal and detailed information.

Trumps in a Spread

Major Arcana cards represent spiritual or universal forces, higher consciousness, the collective, and archetypes. When they turn up in a spread, they could be considered messages from the divine. This may indicate that you are being helped or influenced by powers beyond your own everyday awareness, or that aspects of the reading (or the subject of the reading) have implications beyond the obvious, physical ones. A spread with many trumps in it shows that the matter is complex and involves different levels of being. It can suggest that in order to handle the issue, you need to ask for assistance from a higher power and trust that power to guide you.

Some people view the trumps as indicators that fate or destiny is operating with regard to the subject of the reading. To other readers, the presence of Major Arcana cards means you are seeing the results of past actions starting to manifest in your life.

Trump Position

Notice the positions of the Major Arcana cards. Do they appear in the early or past portion of a spread or toward the end or future part? Do they represent opportunities or obstacles? Do they show areas you are aware of or hidden influences? Whenever a trump card turns up in a spread, pay extra attention to it, for it can reveal a great deal.

You will notice as you do readings that shuffling the cards can cause some of them to get turned upside down. When cards appear upside down in a spread, they are said to be reversed. Some readers simply turn reversed cards upright again. Others interpret cards differently when they are reversed than when they are upright.

Importance of Reversed Cards

Much disagreement exists concerning the significance of reversed cards. Many Tarot readers consider a reversed card to be weakened, so that it has less impact than it would if it were upright. Another popular view suggests that reversed cards depict more negative, dark, or malevolent energies at work. In her book *Tarot Reversals,* Mary K. Greer offers an interesting opinion: "Reversals reveal the esoteric or hidden components, the shamanic perspective of the world, and a place known as the dream-time or inner planes versus so-called 'reality.'" Reversals encourage us to see beyond and through the obvious, and to consider a matter's underlying dynamics as well as its apparent ones.

Whether you choose to interpret reversed cards in a spread or read only upright positions is up to you. You may wish to work with the Tarot for a while before you decide whether to interpret reversals in a different manner, and if so, how.

Deciding Which Spread to Use

Which spread to use depends on the nature of your question and what you want to know. Let's say you've possibilities of a relationship with him or her. If you simply want to know whether you should consider him as a prospective partner, you could use one of the Yes/ No methods earlier in this chapter. Or you could try the Single-Card technique, which will give you some clues to the man's character. Or pick a single card from the deck. A positive card suggests pursuing things further; a negative card says don't waste your time.

If your initial indicators are good, and you'd like to know how to proceed with this person, you could use the Four-Card spread. This describes the situation, an obstacle or opportunity you may encounter, what action you should take, and the likely outcome to the relationship. The Immediate Situation Three-Card spread could be useful, too.

Although the simpler spreads can be used on a regular or even daily basis, the more involved ones deal with larger areas of life and longer periods of time. It's probably best to use these only once or twice a year, unless a significant change has occurred.

Creating Your Own Spreads

After you know what the cards mean and have experimented with a number of different layouts, you can feel free to design your own spreads. A spread is like a blueprint of the reading you are going to do. You can include as many or as few cards as you like. You can expand on standard layouts, or you can design a completely original pattern. You are limited only by your imagination.

Begin by identifying exactly what it is you want to know and what you want the spread to convey. Then organize those issues into an ordered plan, marking each card's position according to what it will signify. By doing this, you are telling your unconscious that you want specific answers to your questions, and you are determining the method you will use to access the information you seek.

Next organize the questions into a card plan. Draw your layout and designate a card position that corresponds to each question. Number the card positions on the plan. How many cards you use depends on how many questions or facets of the issue you wish to have answered. Then choose a layout pattern. The visual pattern of the spread can be varied according to your personal inclinations. You can combine both your concept and your aesthetic sense in the layout.

As you order the questions and place the card positions in the plan, you may decide to drop some questions and add others. Include the readee in the entire process.

You can also design multipurpose spreads that can be used to address a wide range of issues and questions. Base them on your personal belief system or a special interest, if you like. Use your creativity, experiment, and have fun!

CHAPTER 9

HOW TO DO READINGS AND DIVINE THE FUTURE

There are many reasons why a person picks up a deck of Tarot cards and begins to study this most elegant oracle, and no two people will have exactly the same motivation. Whether you choose to do readings to get advice about a pressing concern or for general guidance and personal growth, recognize that you are dealing with a power no one fully understands. Respect that power absolutely and don't fool around with the cards for mere amusement.

Attitude's Influence

Many factors affect the accuracy and clarity of a reading. The state of mind of the person being read for will profoundly influence a Tarot reading. If the querent doesn't take it seriously, or is skeptical, her doubt can set up a barrier between her rational mind and her intuition. If a querent is distracted, confused, or unclear about what he wants to know, the answers he receives from the cards will be garbled or vague.

Your Approach to the Cards

The more urgent your need to know is, the more likely you are to get a direct, definitive answer. That's because your entire consciousness is focused on the matter at hand, rather than being split up into several different areas. Your subconscious, higher self, spirit guides, and other levels of being long to make a connection with you and to impart their wisdom in ways that will help you. Most of us don't communicate very well with the different parts of ourselves. The Tarot provides a tool for opening up those channels of communication.

A person's level of spiritual development influences the reading, too. Someone who is highly aware and in touch with his own inner knowing as well as with the higher realms is likely to derive greater meaning from a reading than someone who has a more linear, materialistic worldview. If you genuinely wish to acquire wisdom, if you see the Tarot as teacher and vehicle for transferring insights, you'll undoubtedly be offered a great deal of information.

It is also possible that if you approach a reading with a pessimistic mindset, you are more likely to get a discouraging reading than if your outlook is optimistic. That's because the future isn't fixed. Outside forces don't dictate what happens; we create our own futures. If we expect a negative outcome, that's usually what we'll get. On the other hand, if we keep an open mind and hope for the best, we'll have a better chance of attracting good fortune. Your life is a self-fulfilling prophecy, and you are laying the groundwork for your future right now!

Ability

The reader's level of ability to interpret the cards will also affect the depth, direction, and accuracy of a reading. Just as a physician's degree of experience and training enables her to diagnose a patient's problems, a Tarot reader's level of knowledge and sensitivity will allow him to bring forth information that is useful to the client. Each reader sees the cards in a slightly different way, based on personal experience, cultural background, mental aptitude, intuitive capabilities, and many other factors. A reader whose focus is primarily oriented toward material considerations and outer-world events will analyze a spread differently than one whose emphasis is on the spiritual dimensions of a situation. Both interpretations may be valid, but they reflect different perspectives. The Seven of Swords, for example, can mean leaving a job that you find stifling, or it can indicate a need to reach beyond a self-limiting philosophy to seek a higher truth.

Remember, also, that people are at different levels of development in different areas of life. One person may be highly accomplished in his career (Wands), but have trouble dealing with emotional issues (Cups). None of us moves smoothly from one stage of development to another in all areas of life simultaneously. The captain of industry who controls the fates of thousands of employees may inside be a little boy who still wants his mama. A woman who does not have a job or career may be possessed of extraordinary maturity in matters of interpersonal relations.

Writing Questions

To get a lucid, meaningful response from the cards, you must be clear in your own mind and ask your question in a direct, unambiguous manner. One way to focus on your concern is to write the question on paper before you consult the Tarot. The physical act of writing your question pins it down and makes it more real. If you keep it in your head, you may allow other thoughts to intrude and convolute the original request.

Take a few minutes to think about what you really want to know. Relax, empty your head of all extraneous matters and distractions. Put all other considerations aside for the moment. Then write your question as concisely and precisely as possible. You can ask for a specific, straightforward, yes-or-no answer or simply request insight and guidance, depending on the situation and your intentions.

Let's say you are considering a job offer. If what you really want to know is, "Should I take the job I'm considering with XYZ company?" don't ask, "Is XYZ a good company to work for?" Even if XYZ is financially sound, highly respected, and fair to its employees, it still may not be the right place for you, or the particular position you've been offered might not be your best bet.

On a sheet of paper, write down exactly what you most want to know and the date, and then lay out the cards in the spread you've chosen. Record the spread on the paper, beneath the question, so you can keep a record of your query and refer back to it at a later date, if necessary. After getting an answer to your initial question, you can ask for additional information. If the cards have advised you to take the job, you now might ask, "What is the most important thing for me to be aware of in this new position?" or, "How can I best succeed in my new job?" or, "What will my relationships with coworkers and clients at XYZ be like?" If you simply seek general guidance, you could ask something like, "Please advise me about the job I'm considering with XYZ." If you have doubts or worries, address them, too. Again, write down each question and, underneath it, draw the spread you've laid to answer it. Continue asking related questions until you've received as much information as you desire.

Sometimes you may get an answer that seems incongruous or ambiguous. In such a case, you could try rephrasing the question. It's also possible that the situation you are asking about may contain conflicting or multilayered conditions. For instance, let's say you asked, "Will I be happy in the job I've been offered at XYZ?" and received a negative response, even though the cards had already advised you to accept the job. Perhaps other dynamics you can't understand at present may be in the works, so that both answers are true. Maybe you won't be happy in the job with XYZ, but will make an important contact there that leads you to another job where you will be content.

The Tarot will usually respond to the most urgent matter on your mind or the one about which you feel most strongly—even if you ask something else. Therefore, if you are thinking about one thing and asking another, the reply might not make sense. Determine what's most important to you and write that down in the form of a question. From there you can make a list of additional questions, if you like, and work your way through the list in a logical, orderly fashion.

The Future, Fate, and You

As mentioned earlier, the future is not fixed. Every decision and action influences what happens from here on. Each choice you make in life is equivalent to turning down a path at a crossroads; where you end up depends on the paths you've chosen in the past. Thus, the outcome signified by a Tarot reading is based on the conditions that exist at the time of the reading. If a situation changes, so will the outcome.

When you do a reading, for yourself or someone else, it's a good idea to stress the fact that the indicators shown in the reading are conditional; they describe what's likely to happen if things continue as they are going along now. If you continue to act and think and feel the same way as you do at the time of the reading, you'll experience the outcome that's shown. But if you change anything along the way, the outcome could change as well. Therefore, it's a good idea to update a reading every few months or so.

Many spreads address the past, present, and future— sometimes the near future and the distant future. Near future may mean a few days for one person and a few weeks for another, whereas distant future could indicate a few weeks to a few months, depending on the situation and the person for whom the reading is being done. As you become practiced at doing readings, you'll come to understand your own time frames.

Some spiritual philosophies hold that everything is happening simultaneously—past, present, and future are illusions. That's why psychics are notoriously poor at predicting exact dates. Now and future are relative terms, and although the cards are good at showing what's likely to happen, they aren't quite so good at putting a time limit on it. Therefore, if you ask if something will occur within, say, a year, you may have to allow a little leeway.

Reading for Yourself

Reading for yourself is one of the best ways to learn the Tarot. When you do readings for other people, you may not be able to follow up after the reading. You won't always know if what you saw in the cards was valid or if your predictions came to pass. But when you read for yourself, you can check the information you get from the cards for accuracy and compare it with actual events.

Setting the Stage

Ideally, you'll want to designate a special place to study and read the cards. If you have an altar, a meditation area, or a separate room in your home that can be reserved for this purpose, so much the better, but any space you can make sacred will suffice. Some people like to enhance the space with candles, incense, flowers, crystals, icons, or artwork that holds meaning for them.

It is always a good idea to silently ask for divine guidance before using the Tarot cards. Some people like to meditate, pray, or engage in a ritual before doing a reading. When you feel calm and centered, begin shuffling your deck. Keep your mind open to receive information. Formulate your question and hold it in your mind while you handle the cards and write the question down if you wish.

One-Card Readings

Ordinarily, unless you choose a fixed pattern of shuffling, there will come a point when it feels right to stop. At this point, place the entire deck in a single stack and cut three times, to the left, using your left hand. Then, restack the cards in the reverse order.

If you are totally unfamiliar with the Tarot deck, begin by doing a simple, one-card reading as discussed in this chapter. After shuffling and cutting, you can either draw a card from the top of the deck or fan out the cards and select one at random. In your Tarot journal, note the date, your question or concern, and the card you drew. Study the card, first allowing images and impressions to present themselves to your imagination. Consider how these insights relate to your question. Then, look up the meaning of the card you selected and compare your initial impressions to the interpretation give in this or another book. Engage your intuition and use your imagination.

At first, your reactions to the individual cards may vary from seemingly nonsensical to extremely profound, or anything in between. No matter what your response is, write it down. Later on when you review your journal (as you should do periodically) new significance will be revealed.

Continue this one-card process until you have worked through all seventy-eight cards in the deck. This may take a while, as you are likely to repeatedly select certain cards that relate to the concerns, questions, and issues currently operating in your life. In time, you'll develop a good sense of each card's meaning and how it can be applied to a given situation. Review your journal or notebook frequently. Compare your interpretations of the same card on different dates to see if, and how, they have changed. Examine your interpretations of the same card in different circumstances. Were your impressions of the Eight of Cups different when your question involved a romantic relationship and when you asked about a family matter? Your personal experience with the cards through doing readings for yourself will serve as your primary source of information about their meanings.

Once you have acquired a working familiarity with all of the cards in the deck, you are ready to do more complicated readings. Now you can progress to laying out three, four, or five cards and start to see how the individual cards relate to each other in order to present a more complete picture. Chapter 8 includes several easy spreads you may wish to use.

PART 3
NUMEROLOGY

For most people today, numbers are nothing more than mathematics, which they either love or hate. But numbers can be so much more—agents for more loving relationships, for more money, for better health, for personal growth, for spiritual awareness, and for greater luck. In numerology, each number is alive, a living energy that flows from and into infinity carrying positive and negative characteristics. When these energies combine, they create the spark of life. In ancient times the magi—early numerologists— became so skilled at directing and arranging these flows of universal life, they could shift the expected outcomes of events according to their wishes. Today, you can do the same and use numerology as a guide to help you make decisions as you seek self-knowledge, establish satisfying relationships, improve your love life, and become more financially successful.

Numerology will help you understand yourself through the wisdom of the numbers. Remember: the numbers are alive, they have personality. Beyond that, they are the substance of life and energy that empowers our spirit and soul. Use numerology wisely; it is the language form of the universe, and it has the power to show you how to live your life in joy and prosperity.

CHAPTER 10

MATH AND THE SYMBOLISM OF NUMEROLOGY

Numbers are the most perfect and pure form of communication. Numbers gave us the tool to expand our universal understanding of what had always been, and to impart that knowledge on the future generations. As numbers have become the journey of creation both in the physical and metaphysical world, they have never lost their earliest values.

The info throughout this chapter and this part tells you about the energy of numbers, which show themselves in two basic ways: physical mathematics and metaphysical numerology. Mathematics and numerology both use numbers—accurately, effectively, and creatively—in a process of learning about and manipulating the environment. We can use both in our continual struggle to improve and enhance human life, making it richer, fuller, easier, and safer. However, the similarities end here.

Mathematics is the construction of physical systems for understanding Earth's physical laws. The purpose of this kind of understanding is to figure out how to get numbers to serve us better through education and application. Numerology is the science of understanding the interaction of energies as they join together into a single unit, a metaphysical system for understanding the universe's bounty of wisdom. By using numerology, we can relate to numbers as living forces, flowing throughout all of life.

Both systems have served us spiritually. So let's take a look at where the paths of mathematics and numerology diverged and how you can use numerology to divine your future.

Combinations, Coordinates, and Equations

Nothing that is now, that has happened in the past, or that will happen in the future will ever be repeated in exactly the same way ever again. In order to work effectively with this law in mind, the early architects of civilization had to use numbers to be able to mimic nature successfully. These attempts could only succeed with the intelligent use of numbers.

Here is an example. A river in its natural course was observed to make six bends before narrowing to become a natural dam, from which animals and humans could drink more easily. Because water became predictably plentiful, herds of animals became regular, making hunting easier. Such observations might be recorded mathematically: the number of bends, the distance between the bends, the varying depth of the river as it progressed to the natural dam, and the accurate measurement of the dam itself. The numbers combined, coordinated, and organized into a system, which could then be duplicated. Trial and error provided the refining of the numbers until accuracy in the duplication was achieved.

Voilà, water as needed, far and wide. That water is quickly put to good use: drinking water is now in good supply, and it will attract grazing animals that may be hunted. Furthermore, a reliable water source is key to agriculture, one of the earliest signs of settlement and civilization.

Nature Is a Great Teacher

Nature is the great author of life and a consistently wise teacher of how to live and survive successfully. Have you ever had the following experience? You have a problem that is really troubling you. You have turned it this way and that and can't get a handle on the right way to proceed, so you decide to take a walk, just to get some relief and space.

There you are, walking along, obsessing about the problem, and your eye catches a bird soaring on the wind-flows overhead. You watch, fascinated with the slight adjustments the bird makes with its wings to stay afloat. Just a little adjustment, and this wonderful soaring continues. Suddenly, your mind fills with questions. "Am I making this problem too big? Am I overlooking a slight behavior adjustment that could easily solve this problem? Is the problem not in this life event but in my lack of creativity in adjusting to it?"

Suddenly, a whole series of insights opens to you. You have an idea of what you can do. You can use the image and inspiration of the bird to improve your life. Now you can hardly wait to get back into the problem to see if your new inspiration works as well as you think it might.

This is precisely the way early humans solved their problems—both physical problems, like how to survive, and metaphysical ones, like how to find one's place in life. Both systems approached and solved problems through observation; people looked to the Earth for the physical and to the heavenly bodies of the universe for the metaphysical. In both cases, numbers played an essential role.

The Power of the Magi

The next important step in humanity's spiritual evolution was the understanding of numbers standing independently as the energy of infinite communication. Humans began to realize that 1 no longer stood only for a lion, a single person, an inventive thinker, or a cosmic person. It also carried aspects of universal energy. When used singly, this energy created 1—communication and universal understanding—and when combined into formulas, it could be shifted and correlated to create states of being we describe even now as magic.

The magi, the genius originators of numerology, led very simple lives. Originally their use of numbers was very simple as well; they did nothing more complex than using numbers in their singular form for mystical insight. When they learned that combining numbers in numerological formulas created metaphysical energetic architecture that they could employ for their own reasons, numerology changed from the freedom of numbers to the confinement and placement of numbers (the mystical architecture) to affect outcome. The progress was the same as mathematics. The evolution was the same. The path that was singular became plural.

In the magi's skilled hands, numbers emerged as infinite life, movement, creativity, and communication with and from the universe. The power behind the numbers from 1 to 9 were understood as infinite energy flows that could be combined by orchestrating the numbers/flows in particular spells. The magi manipulated the numbers' energy currents just as easily as you might solve a simple mathematical equation, such as $2 + 2 = 4$. Numbers and the tribe were never separate, but now they could be harnessed for the good of all.

The numerology developed by the magi had the power to lead the way to understanding the communications of the universe. The magi understood that each number had a different effect in the greater universal context and that the placement of the numbers changes the outcome. They could figure out how to guide people in life using numerology as a tool, just as architects could figure out how to guide the building of safer homes using math. The same numbers now appeared in two diverging roads. Like oil and water, the paths were completely close and completely separate.

The Education of the Magi

The magi training took place in a relationship between a master and a student. The student would attend the master almost as a servant, and the master magi would train his student in the arts of numerology and magic. After enough information was passed on for the student to have a good foundation and a degree of competence, he went into the world. He was expected to lead a very simple life and have limited earthly needs so the focus of his experience would be on the energies of life and manifestation. He was expected to guide others for their own benefit, not his own. This meant empowering others with tools to find their own true inner nature, then providing them with the tools to discipline the negative for the enhancement of the positive, the God within.

Of course, the forces of good and evil are always doing battle with each other in all ways. This conflict took its inevitable toll in the creation of beneficial magi and evil magi. In numerology, numbers are infinite energies with both positive and negative characteristics. This means that good and evil are found in the way the numbers are applied. With the information and knowledge of numbers came the power to help others on their way or to control them for the magi's own pleasure and power. These were very real considerations. Over time, the magi created energy architectures of great power. In so doing, they were able to alter metaphysical reality, just as architecture altered physical reality. By taking the numbers and the values of the numbers, they were able to construct a much larger force and a much larger meaning—the architecture of energy flows.

Learning How to Be Your Own Magi

Now that you know the history behind numerology, you can go on to master the tools you will need to be a numerologist or magi in your own life. By understanding numbers as representatives or individual conduits of the flows of vital, lively energy, you will be able, like the magicians of old, to create the art of placement in your own personal inner world. You will be able to predetermine outcome, and as a result, you will become luckier, happier, healthier, sexier, and more spiritually developed.

You will learn how the numbers are combining within you, right now, as you read these words, in this moment. You can identify with numbers, these flows of liveliness, as they blend and unify within you. Your thoughts, perceptions, and actions are the unit—you yourself—that these lively interactive flows create. By coming to understand the unit, or pattern, and how it animates you, you can begin to understand how to strengthen weaker areas of your flow energies and reduce excessive energy, thus creating balance and harmony within. That is the first and often the only step needed to find and then relate to balance and harmony in life.

As you continue to read on, you will get your own tools. You will be able to follow steps to see your life through the eyes of a numerologist. You will understand how to shift your reality to change your outcome, for numerology is personal growth.

You're the Magi

You come home from a *very* busy day. You have a headache and your mind is racing toward a flat-line state. You want one thing—to sit down, or better yet, to lie down. "Don't speak to me, I'm just lying here breathing, and that's the most I can handle right now." However, you have two kids and their associated needs—homework and bedtimes—ahead of you. You think of the numbers.

You take a look at the "Numbers Are Personalities" chart and confirm that 6 is the numerological equivalent of home and hearth. You think of 6. You draw it in the air, you doodle it. You take 6 breaths. You tap your leg 6 times. You gnash you teeth 6 times. You shrug your shoulders 6 times and stamp your feet 6 times. And finally, you say "Six" 6 times.

Numbers Are Personalities

1	singular
2	relationship
3	balanced fun-lover
4	the solid one, structure
5	the doer
6	home and hearth
7	the intellectual seeker
8	expect success
9	humanitarian
10	all-seeing whole 1

What you have done is shifted the effect of the vibration we identify as 6, which expresses home and hearth and harmony. You have strengthened it, raised it closer to your emotional responses and physical actions, and created an environment where you have rearranged the numbers or aspects of vitality to create an outcome of your choice. Amazingly, you will feel more in harmony with the demands of your home. The kids now seem more precious, the dog so dear. The energy flow of 6 has shared with you a bit more liveliness with which to engage with your home. You will have less irritation, more gratitude, and an increase in soul-satisfying receptivity.

The Magi Approach Is Unique

The numbers are like friends that can assist you, different friends in different ways. It's like putting on a color that is flattering one day, but on the next day you need another color vibration to balance you. Think of numbers like this, and change your life!

Does it sound odd? Try it. Numbers are alive. They carry their presence, their personalities, their unique aspect of life, within them. We need only to think of them, or of one in particular, to engage numerology and create an altered mix of the energy flows that are us.

Numbers Bring Us the Vibrational Opportunity

Numerologists, ancient and modern, see time as a huge energetic vortex flowing from the universe throughout the Earth, spiraling counterclockwise. This is the flow of light or color, the yin and yang, aura, qui, chi, bio-energy, sparkles, or whatever other term you might use to describe it. In numerology, this energy is time, and the movement of time is, of course, made up of energetic flows creating a unit. We are fed, connected, and nourished energetically by this universal flow, which is identified through *numbers*.

We are all made up of skin, bones, chemicals, and spirit (or soul, or universal personality). Spirit is vibration. Vibration is the essence of spirit. Numbers are the expression or identification of vibration. They *are* vibration. Numbers are the language of the universe. It is for this reason Pythagoras said, "Everything is disposed according to the numbers."

Thought and sound generate the movement or action in our physical life, for all action is born in thought. In turn, thought is affected 100 percent by energetic vibration. Because numbers are vibration, it follows that we can alter our vibration through our knowledge of numbers and their individual essence.

Vibration carries on the rays of light the messages and information from the universe on what potential is available for us to create today. Each day is different from any other. The types of opportunities to engage in each day vary according to the information coming in an energetic vibration or light from the universe. One day might bring extra challenges; another day will flow more harmoniously than usual. These interactions between us and our surrounding life, and how we choose to engage these life experiences, show us synchronicity in the most intimate way.

The Symbols and Energies of Nature

When life emerged on Earth, the energies were filled with potential for human development. But not much had been created. The energies were a lively void of raw potential. Even though much more has been developed, we still have ongoing universal support for our continued evolution. We activate this potential continually through intent and action.

As you remember, early humans saw symbols in the nature of the Earth and the heavens, and adapted them. From these forms, they eventually derived the pure language of singular numbers. How did it ever happen that these symbols of numbers became both math, a scientific language, and numerology, an energetic language? And how could it ever be that numbers could provide a language of understanding, a pure and consistent tool for thousands of years in hundreds of thousands of lives?

We do know that numbers have been assigned their mathematical values, but what about their numerological values? Have they been assigned too, or are they inherent in the numbers?

Was the language of numerology created by the human need to assemble ambiguous systems that we can project our own beliefs onto, or are numbers truly communicators between people and the universe? Is numerology a tool for self-knowledge, a skill that enables relationships to improve, luck to increase, and more efficient spiritual development to occur, or is it hogwash, a tool for self-deceit and escapism, with virtually no true value?

A Symbolic Language

As early humans developed the need to have numbers in their lives, it was natural for them to convert the most common symbols of nature, and the heavens that surrounded them, into the needed symbols. Straight lines, circles, semicircles, and triangles were forms found in life. Derived from them, ancient folks realized, the geometric forms could serve as a numerical language.

Circles. This symbol is a line with no end and no beginning. It can be started anywhere from a point of contact, and it completes itself. The circle is a constant flow line of wholeness and completion, simultaneously flowing and completing. Also, the circle reminds us of the shape of our Earth.

Semicircles. A semicircle is exactly one-half of a complete circle. The portion that is enclosed gives the symbol form. The other side is openly receiving the energy of life and experience. This symbol is inspired by the form of the Moon as it waxes and wanes and its changing form during eclipses.

Triangles. A triangle is made up of three straight, intersecting lines, replicated in the formation of the Moon-Earth-Sun triad, constellations, and aspects of nature.

Straight Line. A straight line is not really common in nature. It is a singular oddity in the otherwise rounded world of nature, so its special character marked it as a singular occurrence. A straight line had no center and could extend up and down limitlessly. Actually, to go up and down forever or to have the potential to go either way as limitlessly as one chooses is an apt description of the numerological 1.

These forms were there in nature for all to see, pure forms of communication that needed no further description to clarify the form. Furthermore, they were commonly understood among various cultures; in written form, they were common to all despite language barriers. Simple, consistent, easily replicated, they varied in size, but their meanings remained the same.

Humans needed a form of communication that transcended speech, and they found that using these symbols opened the doors to a new way of communicating that encouraged intuition, inspiration, creativity, ingenuity, and imagination for useful, happier lives. Gradually, as people developed the ability to move from symbols to numbers, each number took on a specific meaning, and numerology was born.

True Intuition

To interpret symbols and numbers, you need intuition. True intuition is not a guessing process. It is a deep inner conviction that something is right. Although what you intuit may make no logical sense, and you may not be able to prove it with facts and logic, it can nonetheless serve you as a guiding light, especially at the turning points of your life.

In fact, the greatest thinkers are those who have been able to use an exquisite combination of intuition and logic to further their ideas and life. Think of it this way: just as you need logic to manipulate numbers in math, you need intuition to manipulate numbers in numerology.

Working with the Nine Pure Numbers

The numbers 1 through 9 are considered pure numbers. That's because they each represent a pure quality or, in other words, a characteristic that is pure (not in the sense of being perfect, but unaffected by any other quality). All the other numbers come from a combination of pure numbers. Just as red, blue, and yellow are the primary colors, and all other colors are a combination of the primary ones, so are 1, 2, 3, 4, 5, 6, 7, 8, and 9 the primary numbers, with all other numbers being formed from them.

In numerology, the other numbers are known as compound numbers, which may be converted back into their pure numbers by adding up their digits together. Hence, the number 10, a compound number, may be expressed as $1 + 0 = 1$.

However, the number 10 is different from the other compound numbers; it contains all the qualities of 1 through 9 and becomes all of them. The difference between a 10-derived 1 and a pure 1 is that a pure 1 is like a beautiful tree in your backyard, complete in itself, while a 10-derived 1 is like the backyard. The number 10 expands the singular in 1 as it absorbs all of life's experiences. In general, each number has three qualities:

- The constructive quality, which is the positive evolving use of the vitality of the number.
- The quality of avoidance, as when one turns toward behaviors that deny true contact from occurring.
- The third quality is when one turns into the destructive (masculine) or the devouring (feminine).

Moreover, with every number there is the following choice of how to interact with the options the energies bring:

- To improve your quality as a person.
- To compromise your quality as a person.
- To wound beyond easy repair your quality as a person.

Yet we still have not yet answered one important, fundamental question. How can numbers be math on one side of the coin and, on the other side, be messengers or carriers of wisdom that bring understanding of our place in the fabric of life on Earth and our place in the universal family?

Flow-Line Energies

Math is mental and physical energy; numerology is mental and spiritual energy. When you mentally decide to draw a line, any line, you are also leaving a "flow line"—a line of energy that flows along the shape of the line you are drawing. Therefore, the shape of the flow line is its essence. This flow line is a stream of energy that is drawn from the force of life, infinity, energy, wu chi, the collective, time, love, the source, the void—it is known by so many names because each culture or belief has a different way of calling it.

As you make a line, the flow pattern that is the line is drawn forth through your intent to create the symbol and distinguish it from infinity. As the flow line expresses itself as the individual symbol, it separates, or flows into distinction from infinity. The flow line expresses its nature through form as it flows onward. It expresses its unique attributes, separate from and yet part of the whole.

It follows, then, that the energetic nature of the flow line of | is different from the flow line that creates 2, and so on. The individual personality expression of each   n u m b e r comes to know itself through the process of its moving out from infinity into its own existence and its own right. In other words, when you are writing a flow pattern, out of necessity it excludes all other options afforded in infinity. By the nature of its exclusion, then, the pattern comes to know itself. Each pattern becomes a singularity in its form and in its content—and then it returns to infinity!

We make a O and a circular flow line is created with the pen, pencil, or brush mark. As the flow line completes, the circle is the living vitality of completeness. Create another flow line, the flow line | , and you have followed exactly the same process. Only now what you have created is singular. It has no center, and it reaches up and down.

If you attach the vertical line to the circle, you do two things. You create a center at that juncture, and, at the same time, you redirect the vertical flow line into the flow line of the circle. Now the two flow into each other, and what has emerged as a result is a heavenly sphere grounded into Earth, 9. This symbol then becomes the language and expression   of   the   spiritual humanitarian who draws from spiritual awareness and shares it with humanity.

The flow lines relate to the Earth and the universe. "Up" is upward and universal. "Down" is downward, in contact with Earth. The left side is the intake side. The right side is the outflow side. Roundness is feminine, flexible, open—as in a semicircle, or complete, as in a circle. Straight lines are masculine, direct, and focused. Following this section, you'll find information on each of the flow lines, their form, characteristics, and their gender, but you'll also find information that teaches you about their three types of behaviors.

Flow-Line Behaviors and Personal Choice

We have to admit one simple basic truth in life. We cannot truly control outcomes—and that includes events, other people, and so on. We can only have complete control over our own responses, and we refine our reactions through what we learned from this life event.

Life is difficult—that is another bottom line—and it is very easy to get lost and very far away from your soul's reason for being in this life. Then, the big issue is this: What exactly is it that I am learning here?

If we can't control outcome or events, and we don't have the influence to make people do what we believe is right, then how do we live in acceptance of life as it is? How do we let well enough alone? How do we go placidly amongst the chaos and haste with the deep inner peace that comes from having that boundary in place that lets us know when to step in and engage to try to affect a situation and when to let it slide past? When do we respond in concern for what is happening without trying to get it to go somewhere we want it to go? These are daily and challenging questions, and it is these dilemmas that give us that negative feeling of being lost, or out of sync, or rushing so fast that life has little true pleasure.

We all need guidelines that we can trust, flexible guidelines that give us parameters with the room within to be truly ourselves. No one benefits from doing exactly what they believe another has told them or is telling them to do. We all must choose our own reactions so we can feel 100 percent responsible in responding to the outcome of our choices. If we follow another blindly, then we give the outcome to them and disengage from our own learning and growth. What we are looking for is responses in the great classroom of life that are ours. We want to create responses that keep us engaged with the parts of ourselves that react to life as worthy, that are worth the effort and capable of reaping true satisfaction.

Essentially, you have three choices: constructive behavior, nonengaging behavior, and destructive behavior. The following descriptions of these three types of behavior may help to clear up for you what your best reaction might be:

1. **Constructive behavior.** You can react to an event in a way that is constructive to your own spiritual, emotional, mental, or physical development. Constructive behavior allows you to engage the aspects of the number that is you in a way that your self-knowledge and positive interacting with the world increases.

2. **Nonengaging behavior.** You can choose not to engage— to react, but in a way that actually hides you from the world. This type of behavior creates a personality that hides one's true nature from the world—sort of abandoning the ship while still riding on it. If you choose this type of behavior, you won't interact in a way that allows equality to exist. This style of relating always brings great frustration, because the eventual outcome is that your life is directed by something other than your self. When you feel like a victim, rejected, unfulfilled, out of control, like you aren't getting back as good as you gave, then you have most likely been interacting with life without engaging it in your true nature. Nonengaging behavior is behavior that seems interactive. Actually, however, it creates situations in which you aren't really giving anything of substance to life. It is therefore impossible for anything of true value to be coming from the experience for you.

3. **Destructive behavior.** People who choose this way of behaving are destructive or devouring. Destructive behavior is what
   happens when the drive of interaction is to take from others or
   direct others according to one's will. This type of interaction
   does truly create, and personal self-knowledge can be gained,
   but it violates one of the most basic laws of life. We have all
   been sent here to have free will to maximize our own personal
   growth. To take away another's free will through destructive
   or devouring behavior is to go against this most basic law.
   This behavior creates a deep soul wound. The power and control can feel good for a while because it can feel like the basic
   truth of impermanence doesn't apply—"We have control!"—
   but eventually it all falls apart. The person is left controlled
   completely by what he or she was using to be destructive or
   devouring. The complete lack of personal freedom that this
   eventually brings creates a true downward turn of the soul.

Each number carries its own characteristics in each of the
three possible behavior patterns. It is up to you to choose the
behavior on your own. This ability to choose responses, to have
that moment where the choice is available and then you decide
which way to go, is the ability at the heart of the value numerology
offers to you. It can be much easier to decide how to create the
outcomes you want if you have ancient wisdom giving you the
tools to better understand your strengths and your weaknesses.

The Flow Line of ◯

- **Form:** A perfect circle and its own center.
- **Gender:** Feminine.
- **Energetic flow:** Starts at any point in its circumference, fin-
  ishes precisely the same point, creating a continuous flow line.
- **Characteristics:** wholeness, completeness, filled with endless
  life of the Earth.

The Flow Line of 1

- **Form:** A straight line, no top, no bottom, no center.
- **Gender:** Masculine; describes the mental.
- **Energetic flow:** The flow line goes up and down limitlessly because it has no center.
- **Characteristics:** Singular, contained, seeking, reaching, exploring.

The Behaviors of Flow Line Number 1

Constructive Behavior:

- Being original.
- Acting with creative independence.
- Acting courageously.
- Matching commitment to willpower.
- Leading.
- Acting from inner force and selfhood.
- Pioneering with courage.

Nonengaging Behavior:

- Acting with positional stubbornness.
- Showing true selfishness.
- Unwilling to accept support.
- Performing actions that lead to lack of stability.
- Bragging with no substance.
- Arguing for the sake of arguing.
- Being unmoving, inert; blustering.

Destructive Behavior:

- Grandstanding: Me, me, me, and now, let's talk about . . . me!
- Domineering, denying others an equal voice.
- Bullying with highhanded, browbeating dictatorship; true tyranny.

The Flow Line of $\supset$

- **Form:** A perfect semicircle in connection at its base with a single horizontal line; its center is where the semicircle and the horizontal line meet.
- **Gender:** Feminine and masculine; intuitive.
- **Energetic flow:** The left side of the flow line gives form and protection to the open, receptive, curved container it forms on its right. The semicircle flow line connects to the strong, grounded, horizontal contact with Earth. Two very different symbols in firm alliance and balance.
- **Characteristics:** Cooperation, understanding, relationship, balance.

Behaviors of Flow Line Number $\supset$
Constructive Behavior:
- Making close and deep contacts.
- Bonding in a deep inner rhythm.
- Acting in a loving and tactful manner, with equanimity.
- Displaying a moderate, gentle, harmonious nature.
- Exhibiting service without martyrdom.
- Acting friendly, being cooperative.

Nonengaging Behavior:
- Acting with ambivalence and self-doubt.
- Showing a low belief in personal power, being extra-sensitive.
- Behaving in a way that leads to apathy and kowtowing.
- Being self-absorbed.

Destructive Behavior:
- Manipulating through sulkiness, bad temper, and lying.
- Acting in a truly cruel, sadomasochistic, devious manner.
- Playing tyrant, victim, and then tyrant again.
- Being sly like a fox.

The Flow Line of 3

- **Form:** Two connecting   semicircles, one above the other; the center is in the middle, where they touch.
- **Gender:** Feminine; emotional.
- **Energetic flow:** Rounding to its left, forming two receptive containers on its right, rocking connection to both the universe and the Earth.
- **Characteristics:** Self-expression, creativity, fun.

The Behaviors of Flow Line Number 3
Constructive Behavior:
- Being truly carefree, with optimism that is based in reality.
- Applying personal creativity to all life, like a natural artist.
- Being an aesthete, with creative imagination.
- Loving social interaction, being a kind friend.
- Being embarrassed of one's own talent.

Nonengaging Behavior:
- Showing silly, superficial behavior; no depth.
- Whining and complaining.
- Gossiping; no attention to personal growth; no sense of class.

Destructive Behavior:
- Promoting intolerance and bigotry.
- Filling others with envy and suspicion.
- Creating distrust and being a coward.
- Being sanctimonious.

The Flow Line of 4

- **Form:** A number made up of four connecting straight lines at right angles to one another; the center is where the square meets the line.
- **Gender:** Masculine; physical.

- **Energetic flow:** Receives from the universe, structures it, and grounds it.
- **Characteristics:** Structure, discipline, reliability, stability.

The Behaviors of Flow Line Number 4
Constructive Behavior:
- Getting organized, having the ability to apply ideas.
- Providing practical and patient service.
- Being able to endure.
- Being filled with devotion and loyalty.
- Being trustworthy, economic.

Nonengaging Behavior:
- Acting dull and plodding.
- Not willing to take risks.
- Being tight with money.
- Thinking in dogmatic ways, being rigid and severe.
- Being restrictive of self.
- Showing a stubborn refusal to budge.

Destructive Behavior
- Loving to destroy with violence.
- Breeding inhuman behavior.
- Lacking empathy.
- Generating jealousy, cruelty, violence through true hatred.

The Flow Line of 5
- **Form:** Two straight lines and a semicircle. One straight line reaches into the mental plane, supporting heaven, the other connects the mental and the semicircle, which rounds on its left and forms a container on its right. The center is where the vertical line meets the semicircle.
- **Gender:** Feminine and masculine; physical.

- **Energetic flow:** A reaching for and a focusing of mental energies; drawing direct, focused movement down to connect the rounded, protecting container rocking on Earth.
- **Characteristics:** curiosity, adventure, shaker-mover.

The Behaviors of Flow Line Number 5
Constructive Behavior:
- Having an active, clever mind; displaying mental curiosity.
- Living an active life filled with versatility and variety.
- Loving progress and personal freedom.
- Embracing life's activities with a sense of adventure.
- Being a great companion and fellow traveler.

Nonengaging Behavior:
- Being completely irresponsible to anyone other than the self.
- Indulging the self, which leads to carelessness, thoughtless behavior, and inconsistency.
- Having base values.
- Pursuing sensation.

Destructive Behavior:
- Becoming corrupt.
- Engaging in substance abuse.
- Being an uncontrolled free thinker.
- Enjoying a complete indulgence of sensation.

The Flow Line of 6
- **Form:** A larger semicircle with a smaller circle curled into it at its base; its center is where the line touches itself.
- **Gender**: Feminine; emotional.
- **Energetic flow:** The flow line curves to the left, containing and securing the smaller circle on its left.
- **Characteristics:** Nurturing, comforting, a number that represents the home and hearth.

The Behaviors of Flow Line Number 6
Constructive Behavior:
- Having a protective, loving nature.
- Creating a harmonious home, within and without.
- Being compassionate and empathetic.
- Believing in balanced, firm justice.
- Giving comfort by bearing burdens willingly.

Nonengaging Behavior:
- Acting in a flurry of nonproductive activity.
- Worrying, meddling, interfering.
- Being a true martyr.
- Giving sympathy filled with pity.

Destructive Behavior:
- Being a constant spoilsport.
- Undercutting relationship with suspicion and jealousy.
- Behaving tyrannically with loved ones.
- Expecting slavelike devotion from loved ones.

The Flow Line of 7
- **Form:** Two straight lines joining on the top at an angle; the upper line is one-half the length of the lower line and horizontal, connecting into the diagonal flow line. The center is where the two lines meet.
- **Gender:** Masculine; intuitive.
- **Energetic flow:** The flow line connects into the mental energies and after taking a sharp turn, runs a downward diagonal course to no apparent end . . . to the devil, if not restrained.
- **Characteristics:** Spiritual, analytical, stillness.

The Behaviors of Flow Line Number 7
Constructive Behavior:

- Having a peaceful nature.
- Being spiritually motivated.
- Loving analysis, science, medicine, and research.
- Having refinement, being elegant, poised.
- Being enigmatic; still, silent.
- Having wisdom.

Nonengaging Behavior:

- Being cold and aloof.
- Exhibiting high-strung nervousness.
- Showing irritability.
- Self-doubting.
- Undercutting sarcasm.
- Acting confused and erratic.

Destructive Behavior:

- Creating turbulence and confusion.
- Showing great weakness to sensation.
- Cheating others.
- Expressing true malice.
- Being devoured by the darkness.

The Flow Line of 8

- **Form:** Two complete circles, one on top of the other; the center is in the middle, where they join.
- **Gender:** Feminine and masculine; mental.
- **Energetic flow:** The flow line is two flows moving in two complete circles, joining in a flow of unification (notice that an 8 flipped on its side forms the infinity symbol ∞).
- **Characteristics:** Complete, unified, it represents the giver and receiver, expects success.

The Behaviors of Flow Line Number 8
Constructive Behavior:
- Having power, trustable authority.
- Enjoying the kind of success born from a just, discriminating drive to persevere.
- Enjoying self-reliance that thwarts dependency issues.
- Showing self-control.

Nonengaging Behavior:
- Being driven by the desire for money, recognition, and power.
- Exhibiting a low level of compassion, tolerance, and caring empathy.
- Creating isolating stress, strain, and anxiety, leading to poor judgment and inefficient use of energy.

Destructive Behavior:
- Being a true tyrannical bully.
- Acting abusive and vengeful.
- Lacking justice and justifying unscrupulous behavior.
- Seeking revenge for imagined wrongs.

The Flow Line of 9
- **Form:** A full circle on top, connected to a line going straight down; the center is where the circle and the line meet.
- **Gender:** Feminine and masculine; a blend of emotional and intuitive.
- **Energetic flow:** A sphere in heaven connects to Earth through a downward-focused flow.
- **Characteristics:** Universal, humanitarian, intuitive.

The Behaviors of Flow Line Number 9
Constructive Behavior:
- Making an expression of universal love.

- Attending to a higher law; serving humanity selflessly.
- Being a magnetic humanitarian who is filled with compassion, equanimity, and understanding.
- Showing a breadth of vision and empathy.

Nonengaging Behavior:
- Acting highly emotional.
- Showing soppy sentimentalism.
- Proving an inability to concentrate and focus all the forces of the 9.
- Being a loose cannon.
- Behaving like a dreamer, no true accomplishment.
- Sitting up in a cloud and deciding to join life when life suits them.

Destructive Behavior:
- Living a life of pathetic dissipation.
- Exhibiting a permissive, immoral character that degenerates to obscenity, total lack of civility, and glowering.
- Acting embittered with life.

The Flow Line of 10

- Ten is a compound number.
- Ten is made up of each of the preceding numbers—1, 2, 3, 4, 5, 6, 7, 8, and 9—and their characteristics.

The Behaviors of Flow Line Number 10

- The 10 will carry the qualities of the preceding numbers, now integrated in a single 1.

The Flow Line of 11

- **Form:** Two single parallel, straight lines; no center.
- **Gender:** None.

- **Energetic flow:** Flow lines are extending up to infinity and down (to the core of the Earth, or to the devil). But because the balance of reaching up and down is maintained, imbalance with the dark doesn't happen like it does with the 7.
- **Characteristics:** Spiritual mastery.

The Behaviors of Flow Line Number ||
Constructive Behavior:
- Spiritual teaching and leadership fueled by intuition, brilliant revelation, inspired invention, and charismatic fire.
- Exhibiting a solid spiritual foundation.
- Understanding that the material world is seen as only the tool for creating options.

Nonengaging Behavior:
- Having no clear, focused direction.
- Being unreliable; uninterested in deep human issues.
- Acting contained, self-superior.
- Imposing beliefs without sensitivity.

Destructive Behavior:
All the crummy qualities of someone who feels they deserve what they want because people are undeserving and imperfect, but the 11 is so much better. These include:
- Dishonesty
- Cruel manipulation
- Degrading debauchery
- Miserly greed

The Flow Line of 22
- **Form:** Two semicircles connected to horizontal baselines; the center is where each symbol connects the semicircle to the base and the synergy that is created.
- **Gender:** None.

- **Energetic flow:** Two very different symbols in a perfect reflective match.
- **Characteristics:** Relationship mastery on Earth, where everything is in relationship; spiritual mastery.

The Behaviors of Flow Line Number 22

Constructive Behavior:

- Living with material mastery and accomplishment on all levels of reality.
- Exhibiting empowerment.
- Being a practical idealist.
- Having an uplifting presence.
- Living with the stillness of inner peace.

Nonengaging Behavior:

- Demonstrating aggrandizing, unrealistic behavior.
- Being unable to find a solid sense of self-worth.
- Acting with scornful indifference.

Destructive Behavior:

- Making power-driven, vicious attacks on others.
- Being scornful, degrading of others.
- Being capable of all aspects of crime.

Every number is equal. Every number is compatible with every other number. Every number has its own path to all the following qualities: compassion, love, equanimity, unity, and acceptance. Every number is completely distinct and in harmonic balance with the others. This ability to be distinct and remain in symphony with the group is called *syntony*.

The Potentials of Completion

It's fun to follow this path one more step and see what the flow lines would be expressing if the pure symbols were completed, like this:

Potentials of Completion

1 would remain the same flow line—singular, limitless potential in either direction.

2 would become a sphere on a horizontal line—grounded completeness.

3 would become the 8, the power of life found through a light and open heart.

4 becomes a square with a single line connecting to the Earth—stability is still the expression and the challenge is to not get closed and rigid like a poorly grounded square.

5 would become a triangle on a circle, a representation of great strength and special gifts—the triune resting on a circle of completion.

6 would become a circle containing a smaller circle—that which is complete, protecting, nurturing.

7 would become an isosceles triangle—perfect strength, perfect form.

8 stays complete.

9 stays complete.

So with the flow lines extended, the possible full personal growth that each symbol represents becomes clearer. The numbers 1, 8, and 9 start complete and work on expressing this completeness in harmony and balance with their life experiences. They're experiencing rest within the structure of the form; much of the experience is spent keeping the flow structure strong, so containment of the pattern is possible.

The others—2, 3, 4, 5, 6, and 7—are evoking more through experimentation in life to discover aspects of completion. With these numbers comes more movement, more seeking from without, an engagement with life on various levels.

Flow Lines Are Guides

Flow lines are indicators, markers, and our guides in life. They existed before we existed, and we harnessed their powers in the numbers we use, both in mathematics and in numerology. Numbers have the power of the flow-line energy to help you know yourself—physically, mentally, emotionally, and spiritually.

As we have grown, changed, and evolved as humans, the universal is always guiding us. As creatures of complete free will, we can develop our potential and in this way expand the self-knowing of the numbers. They guide us, and, in turn, we continue to work on and develop them.

CHAPTER 11

YOUR SOUL ESSENCE AND TALENT NUMBERS

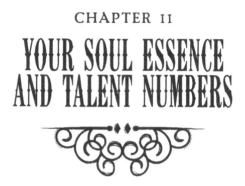

Numerological formulas have guided thousands of people before you, and now it is your turn to receive that guidance. You can use the formulas to determine your soul essence number and talent number as tools to help you expand your awareness of your most basic, most reliable characteristics. What is your deepest characteristic? How can you determine your natural talents? You'll learn how to determine both in this chapter.

Your Soul Essence Number

The first order of your life's business is to determine your soul essence vibration. This is your most important mission because until you have your own energy packaging together, it isn't really possible to bring harmony to your connections to life. In this harmony, you must also be able to have synchronicity, a good rhythm of learning, and balancing support throughout the remainder of your life experience.

Here is the ancient formula:

1. Write out your full name (first, middle, and last) in capital letters. Note, it is very important that you use your true name as you calculate your soul essence number. If you are addressed differently by different people, please con-

sider which name resonates with you most deeply. Also, as you write out the letters of your name, remember that you are working with flow lines, which means you are working with energy. To get the essence of the flow-line vitality, you need to make sure each step is done in keeping with the wise authority of the ancients. Letters must be written out according to the flow-line patterns as seen in the next step!

2. Write the correct root number *above* each vowel, being sure to shape your numbers and letters in the old numerological way as seen here! Here are the numerical equivalents for each letter as well as examples of how to shape your letters using circles, semi-circles, and straight lines:

Number Values of the Alphabet			
A	1	N	14 = 5
B	2	O	15 = 6
C	3	P	16 = 7
D	4	Q	17 = 8
E	5	R	18 = 9
F	6	S	19 = 10 = 1
G	7	T	20 = 2
H	8	U	21 = 3
I	9	V	22
J	10 = 1	W	23 = 5
K	11	X	24 = 6
L	12 = 3	Y	25 = 7
M	13 = 4	Z	26 = 8

3. Add up the vowel root numbers of your first name, middle name, and last name.

4. Finally, add up the final vowel root numbers for each name.

The soul essence number that emerges from this formula can remind and confirm to you the nature of your deepest, most meaningful essence. This is what you came into this lifetime to express, in all the affairs of your life. It is the part of yourself that you long to know about and that you were made to share fully with others. To live life from this center core of yourself is to live from your soul.

Looking with an Ancient Eye

But what does your soul essence number represent? You have two ways of finding out. First, you can consult the ancient masters of numerology, who have compiled this information over thousands of years. Second, you have the power of intuition to look inside yourself and find your own interpretations. All you have to do is meditate and look inside yourself to find the meanings of the numbers, and then see what the masters have left for us as their interpretations and experiences (as the following sections describe).

Soul Essence The Flow Line of 1

This is the essence of one who is here to claim the qualities of learning and giving that are associated with singular contributions. Achievement, creation, invention, family, and friends are expressions of the 1's ability to achieve and create success. The 1 is loyal, a leader who is fair and given to spurts of amazing generosity. The 1 shows and inspires others by personally demonstrating what they are capable of doing as individuals.

Symbol	Possible Behavior
Straight vertical line	Stands alone
Connected up and down	Draws from heaven and Earth alone
Narrow line	Keeps self very singular

The soul learning is to see life as a self-reflector and not as a theater to perform in. In doing that, the balance of appreciating the equality of all things—including the 1—becomes the treasured drop of wisdom gained from the life.

Soul Essence The Flow Line of 2

Soul essence 2 is filled with the capacity and desire for contact with others. This personality loves individuals, groups, communities, nations, and the world as a whole. The 2 essence is a tireless worker for others, who wants to create environments in which people thrive, in which the focus is usually comfort, security, peace, and harmony. The desire to create a better world promotes the ability of the 2 to be diplomatic, empathic, emotionally sensitive to the unsaid words of others. This in turn creates an astounding ability to welcome in all and then more: "Always room for one more."

Symbol	Possible Behavior
Rounded top	Receptive
Straight horizontal line	Very steady
Large container	Lots of space for life and others

There is a natural humility that goes with the 2. This creates a quiet, sometimes obscure life and an amazing ability to be blessed in the small wonders of life. The only rigidity is in the support of others, which 2 will do with a quiet force few will go against.

The learning is to gain the golden drop of wisdom through developing a commitment to a sense of purpose and direction that gives direct benefit to the 2.

Soul Essence The Flow Line of 3

This soul essence is pure light and fun. This is an essence that loves to share and inspire joy and happiness. This tends to automatically draw friends and admirers by the droves. The 3 soul essence draws fun from everyone and everything. Like a happy puppy, the 3 goes through life with ears flapping, tail wagging, engaging, with a pure joy of being alive.

The 3 essence doesn't recognize tragedy and loss as a reason for depression or self-doubt. It is not really true that the 3 essence is a specialist in escapist behaviors; instead, it is more that every situation has a silver lining, and it is this element that the 3 essence sees and relates to.

You will never find a 3 essence holding onto any memory that makes them dour. The victim view is simply not part of their character or how they approach life. This essence is joy of living, and life is indeed a pleasure. The cup is not only always half-full, but that half is bubbling over the top.

Symbol	Possible Behavior
Very rounded	Relaxed and flexible
Balanced, but looks like rocking comes often	Likes to move around 2 spaces for life, can't get enough of life

The lesson that 3 essence can derive from life is to settle down, focus, concentrate, and enjoy life. That means enjoying not just the ripe fruit but the whole process—and that includes planting, tending, pruning, nurturing, and finally eating the fruits of life. This means learning to use patience as a tool for keeping interested in the process. The 3 essence has virtually no concentrated patience.

Soul Essence The Flow Line of 4

The 4 essence is the pure soul of dependability, structure, loyalty, and trust. In other words, this essence is everything you would associate with a firm, solid expression of the best of values, morals, and traditions. Because of the amount of structure that is creating the space, you have a person who is very disciplined—for a cause.

This is a soul essence who upholds the most basic structures or morals of the culture. In the Western world's case, this would be partnership loyalty, family care, a respectable job, and true national support. This soul essence is traditional, not particularly inventive, but very loving. The 4 essence is invested in both needing and giving a consistent and constant support. The 4 soul essence is inclined to see others' needs before his or her own and is therefore capable of putting others first when making decisions.

Symbol	Possible Behavior
A strong structure	Very structured person
Sharp angles	Likes things to be clear and direct
Base much smaller than the top	Receives much from heaven and takes the time to turn this bounty into action

The 4 soul essence will learn the value of always adding to and updating self-knowledge to avoid a limited point of view and holding onto the past. The 4 essence will also gain wisdom on having the scope of self-knowledge to withhold that which cannot be freely given.

Soul Essence The Flow Line of 5

The 5 soul essence is the mental seeker and emotional explorer who is constantly on the move. This essence is restless and freedom-oriented, the shaker-mover energy personified. The constant curiosity makes the 5 essence very adaptable to life but not often really changed by it. Something of a dilettante, this essence adds a special liveliness to any situation it finds itself in.

They are usually ready to move on to the next experience whenever the present one no longer holds the attention or interest of their vastly experiential nature. This natural way of expanding into the full panoply of life's banquet embraces most dearly the arts, music, great food, travel, and fine clothes and jewels. To this soul essence, all these things mean the good life that has been sought, embraced, and fulfilled.

Symbol	Possible Behavior
Strong upper mental reach	Curious mental energies
Strong, structured emotional space	Emotions and drive to success are one
Very rounded, grounded base	Constantly on the move

The learning that the 5 essence will have as life naturally unfolds includes loyalty, consistency, fascination with the process, and a patient acceptance that everything opens, but only in its own time. You can't get a bush to bloom by telling it to.

Soul Essence The Flow Line of 6

The 6 soul essence is the nurturer. It embodies a powerful essence of protective friendship, loyal love, a comfy home, and a deep, steady root that gives endless support to others. So deeply connected to the physical and emotional rootedness, the 6 essence carries a deeply comforting, calming, and reassuring quality that speaks of life as a challenge at times but one that remains eminently trustable. The 6 essence demonstrates to others how to hold back the fear of life's unexpected twists and turns and believe in the power of comfort and sustaining love as an ever-present force to balance the impermanence of change.

Symbol	Possible Behavior
Soft and rounded	Feminine and nurturing
Returns to itself	Keeps loved ones safe
Protected space	Protects

The 6 essence is inclined to work out of the home or in a very homey refuge, a protecting environment, counseling or conducting laws that protect. The 6 essence expresses all the qualities one associates with home in all aspects of life.

Everyone is greeted as a guest/friend and is given stable, loving, parental support. The 6 essence has a great natural compassion and empathy for others. The 6 essence will give tremendous love and support to others. That's because deep within, the 6 essence knows he or she is fully protected and nurtured by spirit. This deep acceptance of protection as a birthright brings comfort and acceptance to anyone in times of well-being as well as in struggle and even in times of peril.

The lesson that the 6 essence will draw from life is to be able to develop a flexible boundary between themselves and others. This boundary will enable them to have a more objective and firm, assertive response to people and life events.

Soul Essence The Flow Line of 7

The 7 soul essence is the most enigmatic or least knowable of the numbers. This essence is always alone, with an involved and evolved relationship to his/her inner world of science, philosophy, and other pursuits of the intellect. It is this relationship that is the 7 soul essence's primary relationship. Because this inner world is the 7 soul essence, he or she is inclined to perform his or her life becoming a living example of the scientist, the philosopher, or the doctor, instead of just being a human being.

The soul essence of 7 is so deeply engaged with the world possibilities conceived in the mental that it is easy to become the embodiment of them. Filled with wisdom, but too inner-related to be easily skilled socially, the 7 essence can give to others vast, intrinsic, and valuable wisdom and be more aligned with the wisdom than the people.

Symbol	Possible Behavior
Strong mental line	Is moved by intellectual inquiry
Diagonal line going down	Goes for the bottom line
Very defined	Loner

The 7 essence loves to examine from every angle. It analyzes everything and hates to be drawn into messy human stuff—fighting, dirty handwork, chaotic environments. With a talent for order, containing a deep and private well of self and an odd combination of spiritual with survival fears, the 7 essence can only be loved if the other person takes the time to know him or her.

The 7 essence will automatically be learning how to be alone and, at the same time, fully content and never lonely. Also, empathy and compassion for the challenge of true-life events will create a more personal attitude with life in general. As the 7 essence becomes more comfortable with life, much of the fear and longing transforms to courage and the ability to find beauty in the wee moments of life.

Soul Essence The Flow Line of 8

The 8 soul essence can be summed up very simply in these two words: expects success. Imbued with talents for organization and systems of any kind, and further blessed with an affinity for large affairs and events and the personal power to conceive, organize, and direct them, the 8 essence has the love of and ability to achieve on a great scale.

The 8 essence will never ask another to work harder, give more, or strive more than 8 essence does. But others should watch out, because they are tireless workers, imbued with their visions, energized by their imagination and projects, and filled with love when they are creating great things. This essence is a power source of hard work to create good.

Symbol	Possible Behavior
Two complete, connected circles	Very complete power
Two circles connected in the center	Balanced
Rounded on all sides	Doesn't collapse under pressure

As life rolls along, the 8 essence will learn tolerance and the balanced hand of justice for those that are endowed with other, very different qualities. They will develop patience with the process, recognizing the goal can only be achieved when the process is well supported.

Soul Essence The Flow Line of 9

The 9 soul essence is the expression of universal awareness and all that universal wisdom expresses. This becomes extraordinary generosity because the 9 essence always feels completely cared for by the universe. The 9 essence's great faith in universal abundance enables the 9 to express a very high order of love. This has to do with sacrifice, but without victimization; sympathy, but without pity for another; understanding without arrogance; and service without treating the person served as a needy, lesser being.

Symbol	Possible Behavior
Upper circle	A higher look at things
Straight line to Earth	Self-directed
Upper circle is complete	Complete universal wisdom

The 9 essence longs to have deep personal love, but this essence emanates such a deeply universal impersonal quality of love that the deep human love is often hard for the 9 essence to really achieve. The 9 essence, who is beautiful inside and out and beloved by most, is often moved to share his or her wisdom in the media to connect with the most people, not for his or her ego but to get the wisdom out.

As the 9 essence goes through life, there will be the inevitable lessons, and these generally have to do with clarity in regard to the abilities and nature of others. Emotional steadiness can become illusive as the 9 encounters earthly challenges. Like Jesus throwing over the moneychangers' tables in the temple, the 9 essence can struggle for emotional steadiness.

Soul Essence The Flow Line of ||

The 11 essence is filled within. This essence carries as a daily teaching and, if evolved at being human, it includes a daily everyday expression of what a spiritual teacher is. In the old definition of spiritual teacher, the teacher stood on the podium and lectured, encouraged, and enlightened the "masses." This is the 11 of yesterday. The 11 essence still has this love of God before its love of humanity, but it tends to express ideals without being accessible as a human being. But the 11 essence is more and more evolving into a deeply human person who glows with amazing spiritual dimension in the blessed, ordinary muck and mire of human life. The 11 essence is a treasure of spiritual teaching and deeply personal human love that ignites the best in all it meets.

Symbol	Possible Behavior
Two parallel lines	Balanced
Goes up and down endlessly	Wisdom from knowing the best and worst
A road space between two straight lines	Knowledge fills it up

As the 11 essence lives his/her life, more and more appreciation will develop for the amazing, even miraculous ways people lead their lives and how the glow of human love empowered by spiritual truths emerges somewhere in every situation.

Soul Essence The Flow Line of 22

The 22 soul essence embodies the characteristics of all the other numbers, including the qualities of the 11 essence, combined. As a result, you have someone who understands the laws of the universe and knows that these laws are only useful if they are applied in harmony with nature's laws. So you have a powerful, practical builder. He or she does not build for personal power, ego needs, experimentation, or from personal insecurities. The 22 essence builds to improve existence on the physical level so all else can grow and thrive. This essence is a true believer in the maxim that in order for human growth and potential to ignite, create, and be grand, the practical, physical aspects of life must be in place. "Care for the body, and the creativity and true nature of the soul will be released."

Symbol	Possible Behavior
Two very firm bases	Very, very grounded
Fits together perfectly	Easily find compatible common ground with others
Two different types of containers	Retains much knowledge and wisdom regarding life

The soul essence, the center of your nature, then expands through other number patterns, each sculpting your energetic flow into life.

Your Talent Number

So, what is this next formula that completes the initial unit you have to work with? It's the numerology formula you use to determine your natural talents. To calculate your talent number, follow these steps:

1. Write out your full name (first, middle, and last) in capital letters. Note, it is very important that you use your true name as you calculate your soul essence number. If you are addressed differently by different people, please consider which name resonates with you most deeply. Also, as you write out the letters of your name, remember that you are working with flow lines, which means you are working

with energy. To get the essence of the flow-line vitality, you need to make sure each step is done in keeping with the wise authority of the ancients. Letters must be written out according to the flow-line patterns as seen in the next step!

2. Write the correct root number *below* each vowel, being sure to shape your numbers and letters in the old numerological way as seen here! Here are the numerical equivalents for each letter as well as examples of how to shape your letters using circles, semi-circles, and straight lines:

Number Values of the Alphabet			
A	1	N	14 = 5
B	2	O	15 = 6
C	3	P	16 = 7
D	4	Q	17 = 8
E	5	R	18 = 9
F	6	S	19 = 10 = 1
G	7	T	20 = 2
H	8	U	21 = 3
I	9	V	22
J	10 = 1	W	23 = 5
K	11	X	24 = 6
L	12 = 3	Y	25 = 7
M	13 = 4	Z	26 = 8

3. Finally, add up all the root numbers together. The result is your talent number.

The Natural Talent for The Flow Line of 1

You are the one who goes forth undaunted. You go where others fear to tread to light the path and show the way. You are the first to be there. This puts you into the ranks of leadership, like this:

- Pioneer
- Inventor
- Originator
- Chief executive officer (of corporation)
- Head of the house
- Self-employed

You spur others to action. You create movement. The force of your pioneering enthusiasm creates the cutting edge for the rest of us.

The Natural Talent for The Flow Line of 2

You are a graceful fit. You make another's companion beautifully. You can understand where another is coming from. You love being in friendship and relationship. Being alone for too long is like walking with one high-heeled shoe on. You excel at people-oriented things and the serving professions, like these:

- Teaching
- Psychic/medium
- Counselor
- Secretary
- Nurse
- Childcare or elder-care provider
- Diplomat
- Networker

Any form of art that has several people in it, like dancing, singing, or writing, is an excellent area of pursuit for you. You would do well as a group leader of personal growth experiences, a massage therapist, or a bodyworker. You provide the environment that is the gentle glue that helps others feel more loved, understood, settled down, and comfy.

The Natural Talent for The Flow Line of 3

You are the spark of fun. You bring the pure joy of being alive to life itself. You are the butterfly who reminds the tiller of the soil to look up and see all the beauty that surrounds him. You are the happy networker for fun. You are the light at the end of the tunnel. You are the breath of fresh air in a stale life. You make a wonderful teacher if you like what you are teaching. The following areas of pursuit are made for you:

• Singer
• Spiritual teacher
• Couture designer
• Creator of breathtaking jewelry
• Counselor who finds better employment for people
• Fundraiser
• Hostess par excellence
• Esthetician/nail and hair care
• Energy worker

You have great personal charisma. Even if you are having a rare bad day, you nourish and refresh the people around you.

The Natural Talent for The Flow Line of 4

You are the solid one, but you're not a bit boring. You bring order into chaos. You make sense out of the crazy aspects of life. You encourage people to have belief in themselves that is practical. You are the glue that binds. You are the teacher of tradition and wise truths. You are the practical contributor to humans. You can be any of the following things:

• Technician
• Accountant

- Professor
- Doctor
- Law-and-order official
- Farmer
- Teacher of older children
- Architect/builder

You're a great organizer and counselor, a gentle leader, and the type of person who understands trends. You provide the foundation, and what's more, you show others how to create one for themselves.

The Natural Talent for The Flow Line of 5

You are the zippy electricity of action. You are the traveler and connoisseur. You are the one who shakes them up and then moves them along. You are action, the Energizer Bunny in life. You like challenge, prominence, and the limelight. You excel at moving things along. The following pursuits are made for you:

- Lawyer
- Politician
- Actor
- Inventor
- Great mayor/civic leader
- CIA agent
- Researcher in electricity, science, and aspects of medicine
- Athlete

The Natural Talent for The Flow Line of 6

You are the nurturer. You are filled with compassion. You comfort, and in doing so, you create security. You are the embodiment of gentleness and a firm hand. You excel at things like the following:

- Alternative and holistic medicine
- Hospital administrator
- Social/welfare worker
- Teacher, especially of younger kids
- Chef or restaurateur
- Bed-and-breakfast proprietor
- Musician
- Writer

The Natural Talent for The Flow Line of 7

You are the mysterious one. You hold the keys to the intelligent way. You are the restless seeker. You can withstand public pressure and unpopularity. You march to the beat of your own drum. You are excellent at seeing out the underside of the issue. You excel at doing the job well and taking the heat if need be. You shine at pursuits like the following:

- Judge
- Lawmaker
- Policy planner
- Lawyer
- Mystery writer
- Banking/financial management
- FBI agent
- Highly skilled accountant
- Artist who works with detail and excellence
- Teacher of anything philosophical

The Natural Talent for The Flow Line of 8

You are the essence of your own personal motto: Love everyone, trust few, and paddle your own canoe! You expect success. You think big, and you think the complete picture. You rely on your own decision-making skill. You inspire others with the overview that leads to success. You excel at things like these:

- Chief executive officer (of corporation)
- Chief information officer (of corporation)
- Financial manager
- Owner of your own business
- Organizer
- Art promoter or patron
- Career counselor
- Fundraiser
- School principal
- Community leader

The Natural Talent for The Flow Line of 9

You are the teacher of spiritual essence as a part of life. You are the natural healer and lover of animals. You are the humanitarian concerned for all. You are the extender of life and faith. You excel at things like the following:

- Minister, rabbi, or spiritual guru
- Mystic counselor
- Psychic
- Doctor of medicine
- Practitioner of holistic arts
- Composer/writer
- Charity fundraiser
- Motivational speaker
- Veterinarian

The Natural Talent for The Flow Line of ||

You have been given the task of expressing spiritual qualities well! You are sustained by the universe. You have a vision for humanity. You have a reformer's hopes and dreams. You are blessed with understanding. You always see a way it can be better. You are the spiritual teacher's spiritual teacher. You excel at pursuits like these:

- Spiritual worker
- Writer/poet
- Minister
- Artist (drawing/painting)
- Chorale leader/musician/choir director
- Charity provider in any role
- Motivational speaker
- Professional advisor

The Natural Talent for The Flow Line of ⅒

You are the builder's builder. You are the practical mover who gets others to produce. You are the heart and soul of stability. You are the manifester. You have a very strong will. You excel at pursuits like these:

- Business executive who makes it better and bigger
- The unifier of the family
- Teacher of how to do it bigger and better
- President/governor
- Leader in world affairs
- Benefactor
- Organizer of community programs

CHAPTER 12

USING NUMEROLOGY TO INFLUENCE YOUR CAREER AND RELATIONSHIPS

In this chapter, you'll learn how numerology can determine and influence your future and how you can use your numbers to your advantage.

Success in Your Career

Your talent number holds your key to success. To focus on this flow line to career happiness, you can use the previous techniques. But it is particularly wise and efficient to work on honing this essence to focus it in the career environment. Look at the elements of your career choice, as follows:

- **The practical elements:** Paper, pen, computer, phone, fax.
- **The mental elements:** Planning, effectively communicating, a good grasp on needed information.
- **The emotional elements:** Good listening, not taking things too personally, the satisfaction of success.
- **The spiritual elements:** The knowing that you are sharing a gift given to you by the universe and that in sharing it, you give back your thank-you; the ability to rebalance from the challenges of personal life when becoming deeply engaged with your career.

For each type of element, use your talent number to enhance your working experience.

Physical Elements

- Organize your desk so that the things on its surface repeat your career number whenever possible.
- Have the form of your career number displayed on your desk.
- Draw your number with the tip of your finger as you are refocusing.
- Sitting at your desk, tap your heels on the floor the right number of times.
- Have a bouquet of flowers with the number of blooms the same as your number.
- Have pens lined up in the drawer. Get the same number as your talent number.

Mental Elements

- Plan your calendar in groups of your career number. For instance, if you are a 2 talent essence, you might organize your calendar and your goals in 2s.
- Stack your books, order your world, and create your open spaces in groups of your talent number.
- To quickly refocus, draw your talent number with the tip of your finger.

Emotional Elements

This requires some understanding of the elements that make up your talent essence number.

Emotional Elements

1 Walk or move somewhere quickly and on your own.

2 Sit down for a quick chat with someone you like.

3 Whip open a good joke book.

4 Think about the great stability of the chair, the room, the building, your bike, car, or anything.

5 Take 5 to travel agent and get some quick information about a future trip you might take.

6 Call a friend who needs some comfort and set up a time to get together.

7 Collect favorite quotes, and either read them or add to them.

8 Figure out how you can work harder more easily.

9 Send a check off to a favorite charity.

11 Write a quick article for that tiny little spiritual press.

22 Do a quick sketch of an ideal planned community.

Spiritual Elements
• Visualize or imagine your talent number, and give thanks for the opportunity to utilize this vibration for your learning and to share with life.

Numerology and Relationships

Relationships are the great knot of eternity. We all long for a rich and rewarding closeness of some sort with something or someone. Some of us have primary heart connections with work or animals or plants. And then there are those of us who as our lives go on are working out the vagaries of communication, chemistry, commitment, and continuity to create heart relationships with other people.

The Most Basic Love
Self-love is like a very personal garden within us. We can plant our seeds of creativity, self-esteem, self-belief, and courage there. We can nourish the growth of these personal aspects. We

can radiate to others our self-love and self-acceptance. But we can never have anyone enter this sanctuary within. It just isn't possible. It is our soul place. It is our most personal and private area. It is the part of us that our reconstructor of self-love returns us to. The magi taught that self-love is the igniter that enables us to love another. One cannot exist without the other, and usually they are equal. The degree to which we love ourselves is the degree to which we are able to love others. The degree to which we love another is the degree to which we love and accept ourselves.

But for that special one, the one with whom we have decided we want to share the roller-coaster of life and brave the Roto-Rooter, we need our ever-present tools to help us on this vital journey of relationship—the acceptance and expression of love.

Receiving Love Is the Miracle

The magi further taught that it is essential to receive the gift. We have so many choices in our culture, such abundance, that it is easy, probably way too easy, to pass from one thing or one person to another without really receiving any gift that is offered by whatever is at hand.

Receiving the gift is the first experience of living—we receive the gift of our life—the bottom-line grounding wire in all life's experiences. If you don't receive the gift, every gift to come your way, you cannot activate yourself to engage appropriately with the experience. You will be engaging only according to your own inner agenda, and that, of course, is repeating a habit, or your karma. Receive the gift, and respond as you choose. After truly receiving, you begin to loosen the ties that bind you into your karma, repetition. Your life task frees you up to work more comfortably with your desire to form and improve lasting relationships. When deepening your ability to be effective with the application of your life task, love will fill you more profoundly. Even in your darkest night you carry an unexplainable feeling of being on target with your learning challenge.

There Are Three Relationship Areas

Numerology can help you understand what kind of gift will be in various different combinations of numbers. If you are looking to find or deepen a relationship with a loved one, you want to work with three different areas between you: compatible, synergistic, and supportive. Compatible numbers, which are naturally sympathetic to each other, demonstrate a need for expression at a soul level. Synergetic numbers act as opposites, bringing the other person the other life view, the balanced opposite. Supportive numbers allow two people to complement each other.

The general rule of thumb is this:

- Relationship of soul essence is best in **compatible numbers**, so if you want friendly ease and cooperation, seek your compatible number.
- Relationship of personality is best in balanced opposites, so if you want a dynamic, passionate connection that never loses those qualities, seek your **opposite number**.
- Relationship of life task is best in **supportive numbers**, so if you want support to find yourself and the other, then look for your supportive flow number.

When you are looking for a valuable relationship or for skills to improve a relationship, it is useful to have an understanding of three different root numbers—soul essence, natural quality, life task—and their best possible connections.

To better understand relationship numbers, we have relationship wheels that visually demonstrate how the numbers work together. You will be introduced to these wheels in this section. Here is what you need to understand about them:

1. The wheels turn counterclockwise because energy works counterclockwise.

2. A 10 is used in the chart because even though it is usually a root of 1, a 10 essence carries different qualities than a root 1 in relationship, and that needs to be acknowledged.

3. All numbers are compatible, synergistic, and supportive, some combinations more than others.

4. Each combination brings a different type of compatibility.

5. These charts show just the root number relationship. A deeper look would be done by studying numerology further or by working with an expert.

6. Respect and appreciation are always needed for the gift— no judgment.

7. The inevitable irritation that will come up is a part of the mix. When you want that person to be more like you, they can't be. That's good, not bad!

8. Each relationship works both ways.

Soul Essence Numbers for Compatibility

The soul essence relationship that nurtures and renews the soul's journey through life is often represented in the easily compatible numbers. The soul requires open depth to be nourished. It thrives in understanding, acceptance, and nonverbal communication. In soul communication, a simple act can speak volumes. The act of nourishing our souls makes the essential challenges of life more possible. To renew the soul is to have life become more filled with beauty.

Renewing the soul in deep human contact makes it easier to rouse oneself to tackle the task of elevating personal quality. It also makes the great demands of the life task easier to reflect upon, stay focused on, and it allows us to have that all-important good progress with the lessons. To share a soul alliance with easy compatibility is an oasis of comfort and renewal. The most easily compatible soul essence numbers are illustrated in the Compatibility Relationship Wheel.

Here is what each particular pair represents:

- **1 and 10:** Each understands the value and struggle of individuality, and each one has a different perspective that lends a slightly different and helpful slant.
- **2 and 4:** Both are stabilizers and have an understanding of how that feels and what the joys and challenges are. Both support and stabilize in different ways, but the gluing quality is the same.
- **3 and 5:** On the move, restless, and experiential, neither wants to slow the other down. The commitment is to now, to the experience, to the truth that emerges in the fast-moving, ever-changing panorama of life.
- **6 and 8:** Successful builders of family and substance, both expect to be successful and depend on outward success to confirm the soul's success. Both bring comfort and protection.
- **7 and 9:** These are the thinkers, analyzers, and the seekers of the culture, dedicated to the betterment of humanity and the discovery of truth through the disciplines of the mind.

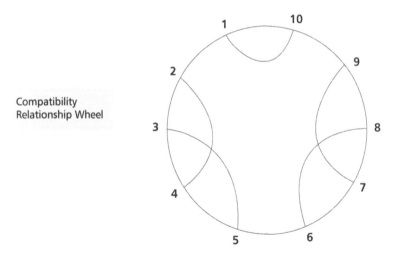

Compatibility Relationship Wheel

Personality Numbers for Opposites

You can calculate the personality number by totaling up all the numbers (for both vowels and consonants) in your full name. When it comes to personality, what you want to look for is someone who is a balanced opposite. You love to read news and stories; he or she loves to listen to news and stories. Each will bring the other a piece that got missed, and thus the whole gets filled in. It is just like the way math and numerology come together, balanced opposites each bringing the needed other half to the table. Balanced opposites are synergistic, dynamic, and never boring. Passion stays, and interest in each other never wanes. Always opposites bring to the table qualities the other needs to complete the journey toward wholeness. The challenge is twofold:

1. Appreciate the difference instead of chafing under it.
2. Don't get lazy and let the other person carry those qualities. These are yours to learn too.

You can see the relationship between balanced opposite numbers in the Balanced Opposites Relationship Wheel.

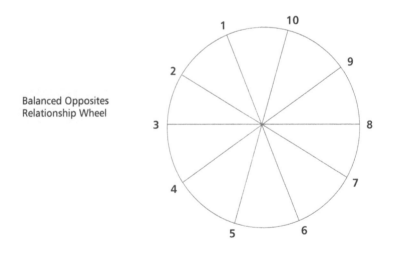

Balanced Opposites
Relationship Wheel

Specifically, here are the relationship meanings in each of the pairs:

• **1 and 6:** The Art of Singularity meets the Art of Union.

- **2 and 7:** The Art of Relationship meets the Art of the Dedicated Mind.
- **3 and 8:** The Art of Pleasure meets the Art of Success.
- **4 and 9:** The Art of Dependable Structure meets the Great Humanitarian.
- **5 and 10:** The Art of Experiencing meets the Art of Seeing the Whole Picture.

Life-Task Numbers for Support

Your life-task number is arrived at by totaling up the day, month, and year of your birth. Supportive numbers are those numbers that with little effort, and usually with pleasure, can support another. This alignment of the numbers is particularly important with the life task. The life task is a commitment to learn something we totally have no idea how to do. It is our lesson. It is how we are progressing our soul's learning. It is the centerpiece of the life, and it is hard. It is wonderful to have a relationship with another who has a life-task number that by its very nature gives what is often needed support to learn a hard lesson through real-life experiences. The supportive numbers are illustrated in the Support Relationship Wheel.

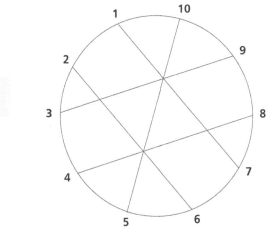

Support Relationship Wheel

For explanations of each specific pair, see the following:

- **1 and 7:** Both are singular and walk their own path. They both know and understand the fun of being unique and the price of being alone. They both are enigmatic and share the peculiar loneliness that comes with being themselves, because no one really gets the 1 or 7 completely.

- **2 and 6:** Both of these life tasks have to do with managing relationships with others. Neither one can be completely happy unless the skill to engage others in relationship and larger union is developed. Both can share the special unique agony of having one's own process so influenced by others. Both support and encourage each other in exploring other methods of relationship and union that may work more successfully for the others, but most especially for the 2 or 6. Both understand the pain of being subsumed in the relationship or union and the challenge of developing the right type of boundary.

- **3 and 9:** Both numbers have a profound interest in others and at the same time an unexpected detachment. Both came to bring up the vibration of the world. Both came to do good work for themselves through others. Both have great personal pleasure in the happiness of others. Both also understand and can support each other in the struggle for continuity, patience with the process, and limits that appear to have no value at all but are there anyway.

- **4 and 8:** The structurer and the builder, these are the confident, dependable numbers that understand the pleasure of steady building and burgeoning success. They both experience great frustration with the flaky aspects of others and wastefulness. Each brings the support that enables the other to move back into the constantly changing flow of life with renewed vigor.

- **5 and 10:** Both see a world filled with great potential. Both feel the drive to engage it and do something with it. Each helps the other to see the wholeness and to increase the intensity of the experience. Neither one likes limits, and when they inevitably occur, the limits will be more tolerable in each other's company.

What about 11 and 22?

The numbers 11 and 22 are, of course, also root numbers carried by a variety of people in all the areas, and they aren't included in any of the relationship wheels because their influence is unique.

Because they are perfecting mastery level in whatever area the root numbers total to, 11 or 22, they are primarily catalytic in relationship. When a single root number is with an 11, spiritual truths and issues will emerge from within that person's nature. The journey involves a commitment to personal growth within spiritual inspiration the 11 creates. Much is true for a 22. The 22 will bring up in everyone their own personal joys or insecurities about creating and building.

Both 11 and 22 can benefit from very close relationship with others. Each person carries a gift for themselves, and in their eyes, each gift is equal. Generally, what the 11 needs from another is warm acceptance. What the 22 needs is a place to relax and wind down for a while.

In relationship, 11 or 22 essence will amplify the spiritual nature of the other person, both sides—light and dark. And the 22 will challenge the beliefs and skills that have to do with building. Each root number will bring forward its best and worst with the mastery numbers. Yup, that's the way it works. We call them mastery numbers because that is indeed what they are. Because they are masters, they bring up all that is their positive essence in another and all that is negative in the essence.

When an 11 and 22 are in partnership, they are dynamite, but must be careful to not burn themselves out.

Because of the catalytic qualities of the 11 and 22, they, more than the other numbers, have to know how to rebalance and contain. But usually, because of their level of wisdom, they can do it.

Relationships are far more complex than a relationship of the primary root numbers. But your basic flow and the basic flow of others are based in the root number. If you get that one worked out, then the nuances becomes easier to work with.

PART 4

PALMISTRY

An intuitive practice that dates back more than 1,000 years, palmistry is the study of the lines, texture, shapes, and idiosyncrasies of the hand. It is not limited to the palm area alone, but also includes the fingers, knuckles, wrists, mounts, joints, and overall shape of the hand itself. Palmistry can tell you the past, but it can also tell you about future possibilities. As it is practiced today, palmistry offers a complete personality profile of an individual, including his or her major life choices, challenges, and opportunities.

With the information found in this part, you'll learn how to read palms for yourself, your family, and friends. This part will help you see, perhaps for the first time, the blueprint of your own life and will also offer understanding and insight into the lives of others around you. You will see striking correspondence between the lines on your hand and the paths you've already chosen. You will discover what lies ahead in the creases and seemingly insignificant markings on the palms of both of your hands.

But while your hands contain helpful information about your talents, emotions, dreams, and spirituality, you should always remember that there is not always a clear-cut, predestined path. The road ahead will certainly have some forks and crossroads, and it will be up to you to decide where you want to go. However, with the help of palmistry, you can embark on your life's journey with a map of your destiny—right in the palm of your hand!

THE APPEARANCE OF THE HANDS AND FINGERS

Before the palm reader looks at the lines on your palm, he or she will make careful observations about your hand and fingers—their shape, texture, and overall appearance. The information that can be gleaned from these observations can tell a lot about a person. In this chapter, you will learn how to interpret the symbolism behind various aspects of the hand and fingers.

Overall Appearance of the Hand

Before taking a deeper look into the lines on the hand, you should always begin with an overall assessment of the hand itself. Hands come in a wide variety of shapes and sizes; to get a clear picture of the personality type you're dealing with, it's important to start with a good reading of the more general aspects of the hand's outward appearance.

Here are the main aspects of the hand you'll want to examine closely as you begin your palm reading:

- **Size.** In general, people with small hands tend to act quickly and perhaps impulsively; those with very small hands are generally free, independent-minded thinkers. On the other hand, those with larger hands tend to be more methodical and thoughtful about their big decisions in life. People with average hands are easygoing—they react according to each situation and its own unique circumstances and are not as predictable.

- **Color or consistency.** Color represents life or vitality. If the palms are pale—white, gray, or even bluish—there are definitely health challenges (most likely circulatory in nature); red hands mean you are quick to anger; yellow, jaundiced hands mean you have a pessimistic outlook; and pink hands mean you are well-balanced and have a healthy outlook.
- **Thickness.** Tilt the hand sideways and look at its width. Is it thin or thick? Thick hands belong to easygoing, noncompetitive people; thin hands belong to goal-oriented, driven, or ambitious people who are on a specific mission in life.
- **Texture.** Fine, soft skin indicates refined tastes and usually belongs to the culturally or artistically inclined. Firm skin shows a healthy blend of physical and intellectual pursuits. Coarse, rough, or scaly skin indicates a more adventuresome, outdoorsy type for whom gloves (and personal well-being) are an afterthought.
- **Movement.** How does the hand move? Does it seem flexible? If it is, the person is also likely to be flexible in his or her thinking and general demeanor. A general rule of palmistry is that the stiffer the hand, the stiffer the demeanor. Have you ever noticed a person with hands so stiff they almost seem mechanical? People with hands this stiff typically have mental or emotional difficulties, or have a hard time trusting others.

Take notes about each of these items. As you get deeper into the lines, ridges, and mounts of the hand, you'll want to look back at your initial assessment to see how developed it's become.

Examining the Hand Spread

The spread of the hand tells you how you are perceived by others. When you turn your hands around so that the palms face outward, look closely at the spread of your fingers. Very close fingers connote a person who is very traditional and overly sensitive; fingers held further apart represent an unconventional, nontraditional thinker.

And what about the other fingers and their positioning on the hand? If all of your fingers lean toward the palm, you are possessive, reserved, and possibly even stingy. If they point outward toward the sky, you can be overly permissive and give until it hurts. A wider-than-usual gap between the thumb and first finger also connotes extreme generosity.

Look at your fourth (little) finger as it relates to your hand. Is it farther apart than the other fingers? Usually, a little finger that points outward and is spaced significantly apart from the third finger means that you have a quick temper and are not to be reckoned with when upset! If your index finger seems to be spaced farther apart from the other fingers on your hand, you have strong leadership potential and can be a trendsetter.

Your Hand's Shape

The general shape of your hand tells a palm reader a lot about your general character. The easiest way to get a quick read on someone is to look at the shape his or her hands form—and to correlate each shape with a particular personality type. In palmistry, there are four basic shapes and one hybrid or mixed shape.

The Conical or Artistic Hand

Conical hands are round, sensual, and feminine in appearance. People with these hand shapes typically have a deep appreciation for the arts or, if the hands feature lots of curved lines, are artists or creators themselves. Quiet, sensitive, and imaginative, they are nonviolent people who seek solace through music, art, literature, and love. The conical hand is called the Air hand, since this element most closely captures the free spirit of the type.

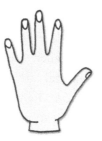

Conical (Air) hand

The Pointed or Psychic Hand

Long, delicate, and tapered fingers that characterize the pointed hand lead palmists to conclude that the fingers point to spiritual truths. This is why the pointed hand is always referred to as the psychic hand—and, in truth, the vast majority of those who have pointed hands do have psychic or intuitive ability.

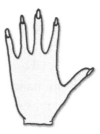

Pointed (Water) hand

If your hands are pointed and you don't think you are the least bit psychic, it could mean that you have the power but have chosen not to develop it at this point in your life. Whether or not you become a psychic practitioner in the future, your intuition and creative energy are already powerful, and you tend to have a tremendous amount of compassion or empathy for others. Pointed hands are often called Water hands because of their deep sensitivity and intensity.

The Spatulate or Action-Oriented Hand

If your hand is narrow at the wrists, but wider toward the fingertips, you have what is called the spatulate hand. You are action-oriented and love unusual adventures; it's not unlike you to pack your bags and head to India for a spell, and then go on a skiing trip to Colorado the next month.

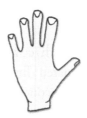

Spatulate (Fire) hand

An explorer of people, places, and ideas, you are daring, energetic, and fearless, often challenging the ideas or positions of others who aren't as open-minded as you. Your energy is boundless; you tend to leave others breathless, unable to catch up with you. Spatulate hands are often called Fire hands, since that element most closely captures the personality traits of vitality and dynamism.

The Square or Practical Hand

A square hand appears to form a perfect square from the finger bases to the wrists. People with square hands are smooth, easygoing types who are very practical in nature and have a realistic outlook on life. They are rooted in their daily lives, and while they are friendly and outgoing, they also have a tendency to evaluate every situation as black or white, with very little left to interpretation. Still, because they are so sensible and level-headed, family and friends regularly seek them out to help mediate or settle volatile situations.

Square (Earth) hand

Square-handed people are most often drawn to careers that require hard work and persistence, since they excel in tackling large and difficult projects. Because they are practical and down-to-earth, these people are said to have "Earth" hands. With the square-handed, what you see is what you get!

The Mixed Hand

Although it's quite a rarity, every once in a while you'll see a hand that has elements of two or more of the five shapes and types. Palmists call these hands mixed. For an accurate reading of a mixed hand, you'll need to look for the dominant feature of the hand.

Mixed hand

For instance, if you see that the palm itself is basically square but the fingers are long, it could mean that the person seems by outward appearance to be dreamy and intuitive, but that inwardly they are actually strong, practical, and even-minded. If all seems balanced in the hand, your mixed-hand person is completely versatile and has a steady, go-with-the-flow kind of attitude. Both temperaments have their positive and negative sides, but there is much to learn from the mixed-hand balanced individual.

Knuckles and Angles

Now, make a fist and look closely at the ridges that your knuckles make when your fist is closed. Do you see lots of peaks? A full "mountain range" with peaks and valleys shows a person who has good health, is adventuresome, and fights for his or her beliefs.

If your knuckles are smooth and even, you are intuitive, impulsive, and dreamy. If they are knotty and rough-looking or heavily ridged, you are extremely decisive and not easily swayed by hard-luck stories. Tiny bumps on the knuckles connote a shy, introverted personality.

Palm Marks and Patterns

In addition to major lines, the palm contains lots of smaller lines and other markings. Now that you have a good sense of the feel and texture of your palm, take a deeper look at the skin patterns on it. Do they form any particular shapes? There are thirteen basic markings that can appear on the palm of the hand, and each has a special meaning:

1. **Chains:** Someone who is "bound" by worry.
2. **Islands:** Loss through difficulty or challenge.
3. **Dots:** Indication of a surprise or a shocking event.
4. **Branches:** Rising branches are a sign of good fortune; branches falling toward the wrist are a sign of potential failure.
5. **Broken lines:** A shift or change in life, or an inability to see things through.
6. **Forks:** Choices pertaining to whichever major line is closest (heart, head, or life).
7. **Circles:** Usually, circles predict great fame and fortune; however, you will rarely encounter them.

8. **Triangles:** Portend great psychic or spiritual abilities.
9. **Squares:** Ability to teach, motivate, or inspire others.
10. **Crosses:** Obstacles or blockages on the way; burdens that may hold you back from achieving your dreams.
11. **Tassels:** Not typically seen on the hand; can represent scattered energies or unmanifested ideas.
12. **Grilles:** Represent lots of starting and stopping with respect to life's endeavors.
13. **Stars:** The most auspicious markings on the palm; people with stars usually achieve tremendous fame—or lasting notoriety.

Typical markings on the palm

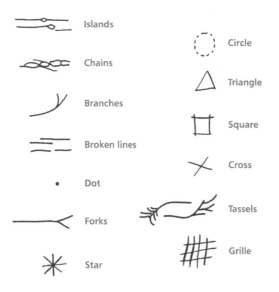

Islands

Circle

Chains

Triangle

Branches

Square

Broken lines

Cross

Dot

Tassels

Forks

Grille

Star

The Appearance of Your Fingers

Beyond the palm, fingers have stories of their own to share. Each finger represents a different talent, interest, or ability. Let's spend some time doing a general reading of your fingers.

Every Finger Has a Name

You may just think of them as your fingers, or tools you use to retrieve things or communicate with others, but in palmistry your fingers are known by their individual, more esoteric names, which correspond with the gods of Roman mythology for their attributes.

Finger Tips Regarding Jupiter

The Jupiter finger is your index finger; it describes your leadership abilities and assertiveness. If the Jupiter finger extends to the base of the nail of the neighboring Saturn finger, you likely have a love of power and a desire to lead others. If it is as long as the Finger of Saturn, though, you can be extremely egotistic and seek to control or overpower others in an unhealthy way. A crooked or bent Jupiter finger shows a tendency to dominate others through unfair means or advantage, while a short Jupiter finger indicates a dislike of personal responsibility.

Sad, Sad Saturn Finger

The Saturn finger is your middle finger; it describes moods as well as responsibilities. This finger can be a prime indicator of depression. If it is noticeably longer than the others, there is a strong tendency toward depression. A shorter Saturn finger can mean you are generally free from serious depression, but that you are fearful of responsibility and have a tendency to bury your head in the sand when a situation carries the slightest bit of pressure. If your Saturn finger is crooked or bent, you have a real chip on your shoulder—possibly even a persecution complex. As a rule, the finger of Saturn is practically never set low.

Apollo's Fire—and Fame

The Apollo finger is your ring finger; it is an indicator of happiness or contentment, and can also show an interest in the arts or sciences. The finger of Apollo also shows your potential for fame. If it's long, you would like to be a celebrity, particularly in the creative arts; if it is excessively long, it indicates a craving for notoriety at any price. If your Apollo finger is short, you shun any kind of notoriety or publicity and prefer to keep a low profile, often working behind the scenes. A low-set Apollo finger means that while you may have an interest in pursuing an artistic career, you may not have been born with the talent to make it happen.

Mercury's Balancing Power

The Mercury finger is your fourth or little finger; it shows how creative or emotional you are. This finger also holds the balance or abuse of power. If it's long, you have the shrewd ability to exploit the skills and talents of others for business purposes. If it is extremely long, extending past the base of the nail of Apollo, you can be a bit of a hypocrite. A short Mercury finger means that you have an inability to use your own talents to the fullest, but don't like to capitalize on the talents of others. If your Mercury finger is set low, you are likely the imaginative, dreamy type—both of your feet are up in the clouds, making it difficult for you to earn a sensible living.

Not All Thumbs

The thumb is one of the most important character divulgers on the hand. It shows your degree of self-control and personal willpower, as well as your disposition, and should always be read together with the head line.

The length of your thumb is significant. A long, well-formed thumb indicates a strong will and sound judgment. A short, thick thumb means you can be quite contrary or stubborn—it's your way or the highway, and opposition from others only tends to make you more convinced that you are right.

The Right Angles

Let's look at the angle at which your thumb joins your hand, since this has direct bearing on your sense of justice and fairness. When it's close to the palm, at an acute angle, you have a more conservative nature and believe that everything should be viewed in terms of black and white. You just don't like to dive below the surface—your reality can be cut with a fork and knife. You follow the rules, pay your bills, and move on to the next experience.

The more idealistic types have a thumb that forms a right angle with the palm. If this is how your thumb is positioned, you are much more willing to see things from other perspectives, and have a strong sense of justice that leads you to give others the benefit of the doubt. Innocent until proven guilty is your credo—and you will always look for the positive in every problem or situation.

Thumb at an acute angle

Thumb at a right angle

Other Types of Thumb

Also note what the top of your thumb looks like. The "waisted" thumb looks like it has a waistline, formed by the narrow joint that connects the second phalange to the top of your thumb. This type of thumb represents an unwavering tact and the ability to understand lots of different viewpoints. If you have a waisted thumb, you're very empathic and relate well to others. You probably volunteer in a capacity where you are supportive of others. You are enviable in the sense that you have a good balance between your creative and practical sides.

A waisted thumb

If your thumbs are squared off at the top and shaped like a hammer, you are likely to be into excess of one sort or another: perhaps you shop, eat, or drink too much. The challenges associated with this shape can be overcome in life with a healthy balance, so learn to pace yourself!

A hammer thumb

Which Way Do They Go?

Now that you've examined your thumb, how about the four fingers? Hold your palm in a normal, relaxed position. Which way do the fingers seem to lean? Is one finger more dominant than the others? Note which one is more dominant and be sure to review this finger's meaning, since it obviously marks your most dominant personality characteristics.

If all of your fingers incline toward your Jupiter finger, you are a highly ambitious person. If all of your fingers lean toward your Saturn finger, you are a person whose life is very melancholy. You have an almost gothic desire to be different from others, and usually set yourself apart from them in negative ways that assure you of solitude. Believe it or not, many comedians have fingers that lean toward a dominant Saturn finger, proving that laughter can overcome sadness with some ambition and hard work.

If your fingers lean toward your Apollo finger, you are passionate in your pursuit of an artistic or creative profession, and you have your heart set on becoming well known for your talents. If all fingers point toward the Mercury finger, you have incredible business acumen and should pursue entrepreneurial interests, especially if your Jupiter finger is long and slender.

Finger Shapes and Meanings

Just like the five hand types, the fingers can be shaped in five different manners, each having a separate and distinct meaning in palmistry. The four basic shapes and their corresponding meanings are:

- **Conical:** These are the fingers of wise, old souls who possess terrific insight and inner knowledge, as well as creativity; these are great friends and supportive people.
- **Pointed:** These fingers point to expensive, eclectic tastes and a great eye for style and décor. Those with pointed fingers are also deeply spiritual and intuitive.
- **Spatulate:** These fingers indicate predominance of the intellect; people with spatulate fingers tend to be witty and interesting, with many layers to their personalities. They are also serious workaholics and can be obsessed with success—but they always make time for serious adventure.

- **Squared:** These fingers signal the need for simplicity and are common with people who are direct, fair, and considerate. These folks are quite willing to work hard for what they want in life, making them ideal business people who lead by positive example.

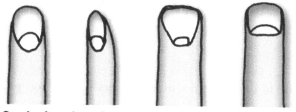

Conical, pointed, spatulate, and square fingers

Mixed finger shapes are very uncommon; a person whose fingers have elements of two or more shapes have a tendency to be unpredictable—they show one side of themselves to the outside world, and have another side that is distinctly different and completely private.

Finger Length

Now, let's move on to length and its meaning. The total length of a finger can be measured from the center of the knuckle to the tip of the finger. A finger is considered to be short if it doesn't reach the joint immediately below the nail on the next-longest finger. A finger is long if it exceeds this joint in length and extra-long if it is the same size or larger on what is usually the next-longest finger.

As a rule, short-fingered people are interested only in quick results. They can see people or situations with broad perspective. If the hand has a strong thumb, a long first finger, and a solid head line, short fingers can have quite a capacity for work and don't mind "pulling the wagon" or doing their fair share of work.

Long-fingered types absolutely adore details and are good "idea" people. If your fingers are unusually long, similar to the pointed or psychic type of hand, you are likely a person who gets so wrapped up in ideas and possibilities that you never act on them.

CHAPTER 14

THE MOUNTS OF THE HANDS AND FINGERS

The palm is divided into nine mounts—raised or puffy sections that contain information about natural abilities, traits, or personal characteristics. If you want to know where a person's primary or dominant energies are directed, look for the most dominant raised area of his or her palm.

Peaks and Valleys of Your Hands

To examine the peaks and valleys of your hand, raise your hand, palm up, to your eye level—you will notice that some areas of the palm stick up, some more distinctly than others. For instance, the cushion closest to your thumb may be especially puffy, or the cushion nearest your wrist might be more noticeable than the others on your hand.

Whatever the particulars on your own hand, you should know that in palmistry those cushionlike developments on the edges of your hand and near your fingers are called mounts. The interesting thing about mounts is that no matter what else changes in your life or in the actual lines on your hand, your mounts will not change. Even if you make a major shift in your career, love life, or personality, your mounts will be exactly as you see them at this moment.

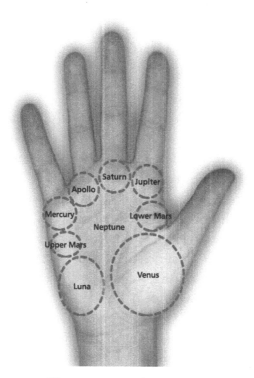

Nine mounts of the hand

Your mounts represent the focus of particular energies in your life, and a dominant mount on either the palm or a finger means that more of your energy is focused on that aspect of your life. The mounts of the palm correspond to planetary energies—each of which, not surprisingly, is associated with a particular character trait.

The Mount of Venus

Because it is so closely associated with your capacity for love, affection, desire, and romance, the mount of Venus is the most popular area of scrutiny by a professional palm reader. When they have their palm read, most people want to know what kind of lover they are, who would be the perfect match for them, and other details pertaining to their love lives. The mount of

Venus, which is located at the base of your thumb, can be a good indicator of how deeply or passionately you love others.

Tendency Toward Passion

If your mount of Venus is overly puffy, it can indicate a tendency toward promiscuity as well as fear of commitment. Just being aware of this tendency can go a long way toward averting its potential for negative consequences.

The exception to this rule is when the head line and the thumb are both strong and steady; in this case, your passionate nature will be tempered by a sound, moral ability to size up sexual situations for what they are—and to escape the emptiness of one-night stands. Instead, you will likely focus your passionate energies into providing a life of luxury and fulfillment for your perfect mate—turning your physical passions into material ones with real and achievable goals behind them.

Of course, love of material pleasures comes at a price: You might find that in your quest to provide a wonderful life for your spouse or significant other, you are less inclined to remember those sweet little gestures that keep the flames of love alive. If you find yourself overlooking romantic love, you need to work harder at keeping a balance between material and physical pleasures!

If you don't have a well-developed head line or thumb configuration, an exaggerated mount of Venus can indicate a callous, uncaring tendency toward instant gratification.

The Venus-Blessed

In general, people with a predominant mount of Venus fall into a physical type with round faces dominated by large "doelike" eyes and voluptuous lips, while other facial features tend to be smaller than average. They are usually slightly taller than other types, and most often have a very robust, healthy outlook on life. Venusians are, of course, the most sensual and socially outgoing of the mount types. They know how to live passionately—and well.

Do you have a love of the finer things in life? Is your home filled with lots of soft, sensual accessories mixed with very special works of art? Take a look at your mount of Venus—more than likely, you'll notice a predominant mount. Since they have such a keen understanding of human emotion, Venusians make excellent psychologists, teachers, and even politicians.

Smooth Operator

What if your mount of Venus is not well developed? A nearly smooth Venus mount can indicate a calculating and overly critical disposition. For these types, beauty is almost offensive, since they are acutely aware that it is only skin-deep. Still, if you have other positive aspects to balance out your palm, you will probably be more of a kindhearted lover than a hot-and-heavy one. Is this a bad thing? No, especially when you consider that physical passion wanes after a time.

If your palm places you in this category, look for a partner whose mount of Venus is similar to yours; though opposites can attract, they don't always stay together for the long haul. A couple with small mounts of Venus can find lasting love together simply because neither sees physical passion as a requirement of the relationship.

The Mounts of Mars

While Venus represents the forces of love and peace, the mounts of Mars represent the energies of aggression and courage. By examining these mounts, you can find out if a person's primary response to challenging situations is fight or flight.

There are actually two mounts associated with the action planet of Mars: the mount of Upper Mars (located on the outside area of your palm, just under your little finger) and the mount of Lower Mars (that area in between your thumb and index finger). Lower

Mars shows your capacity for physical strength or endurance, while Upper Mars tells the story of your moral code. The mounts of Upper and Lower Mars are sometimes referred to as the mount of Mars Positive (Upper) and mount of Mars Negative (Lower).

Life on Upper Mars

A well-developed mount of Upper Mars indicates that you are somewhat confrontational. Fortunately, that negative quality can be turned into a positive one when a crisis arises. And an overdeveloped mount of Upper Mars can mean that you are a bit of a bully—someone who uses physical force to get a point across. You are especially competitive when playing games or participating in sports. Watch out for this tendency—try meditation or yoga to balance this kind of negative energy, and remember that words can hurt as much as physical force.

If the opposite is true and the Upper Mars mount is smooth or not well developed, you dislike confrontation and look for ways to escape stressful situations. Since your strategic and survival skills are superior, you are very good at defending others and can make an excellent defense attorney. Fighting injustice suits your personality and mount type well.

Life on Lower Mars

People with a mount of Lower Mars that isn't well developed tend to have a cowardly nature or may simply be afraid of confrontation. This is not inherently a bad thing, but it could make you much more cautious than you should be in certain situations, and definitely less assertive than you need to be in life. If, on the other hand, your Lower Mars mount is overdeveloped, you may have an overly confrontational and even combative personality. Ideally, your mount of Lower Mars is well developed and more evenly balanced than these two extremes.

If You Are Predominantly Martian

In general, hands sporting a predominant mount of Mars (whether Upper or Lower) can signal a personality type that's quite forceful and dominant in heated discussions—you wouldn't want to find yourself on the bad side of a Martian. Still, even if they are difficult people when they are challenged or frightened, Martians can be fun-loving individuals. Martian types love to engage in lengthy discussions about any hot topic of the day, and are usually intelligent and social.

Martians typically do well in business and commerce; however, those with predominant Upper mounts have an easier time climbing the ladder to success than their Lower-mount counterparts. Physically, Martians are distinguished by their long, angular bone structure combined with a large mouth and a beaklike nose set between strong cheekbones.

The Mount of Luna

The mount of Luna is symbolic of imagination, intuition, and creativity; it is located directly across the hand from the mount of Venus. The normally developed mount of Luna shows a well-developed imagination and a passion for nature, travel, poetry, art, and literature.

If your mount of Luna is overdeveloped, you might have some difficulty in dealing with reality because your imagination gets in the way. If your Luna mount is underdeveloped, you are perhaps just as likely to process every new experience purely from a sensual, feeling standpoint—keeping logic and clear decision-making at bay.

If your mount of Luna is larger toward the wrist area (as opposed to near the thumb), you possess much in the way of intuitive power and can see well beyond the physical reality of life. You know things before they happen and are adept at planning your life accordingly.

Creative, Sharing Types

In general, people with strong Luna mounts on their hands are dreamy, imaginative, creative, and giving. They are very compassionate and helpful to others; often, they are quite protective of the people they care about. The Luna folks especially love to share their special creative gifts as writers, painters, or speakers. They make terrific psychics, artists, writers, or composers. And if a large Luna mount is coupled with a prominent Venus mount, the person is destined for world renown and acclaim.

Since the Moon rules the tides, those with predominant Luna mounts love the water and anything associated with it. If you have this Moon mount type, you probably live near the ocean or frequently travel there.

The Luna Hermit

If your mount of Luna is not well developed or is smooth or unnoticeable, you prefer to stay near home and have a tendency to live in your own little shell. If you do have any imagination, it's a secret that only your private diary will reveal!

Notable Mount Marks

Mounts of the palm often display auspicious and/or inauspicious markings. Mount markings are cloudlike in the sense that they form symbols or pictures but may not be as perfectly formed as an artist's rendering. Although these same formations can occur all over the palm, it's important to note that, on the mounts of the palm, these marks have distinctly different meanings.

There are five main markings that typically occur on the mounts of the palm. Generally speaking, crosses and grilles represent negative signs, while stars can indicate good luck (especially with money) and squares lessen the impact of negative signs. A triangular mark on a mount of the palm shows wisdom.

- **Grilles on the Venus Mount:** Most often, grilles (mixed lines, both vertical and horizontal) that appear on this mount represent lots of misguided or splintering energy. Are you passionate about too many things? Grilles warn you that too many passions can lead to stress, tension, and an unhealthy intensity in your emotions. You will have to balance this energy with calming walks, meditation, or prayer—otherwise, you might be a heart attack waiting to happen!

- **Stars or Crosses on the Luna Mount:** Not surprisingly, the star usually appears on the mount of Luna, and it carries with it a travel warning, as does a cross on the same mount. Be extra diligent when you travel; you can only let your guard down if the star or cross mark on your Luna mount is encased in a protective square marking.

- **Markings for Lower Mars:** Here, the most common marking is the cross, and it signifies that you might have some adversaries out there seeking to do you harm. Could it be that they just want to undermine your credibility, or are they secretly plotting more drastic measures?

- **Markings for Upper Mars:** If you have the lucky triangle on the mount of Upper Mars, you will be able to outwit any potential adversary because you likely possess the skill to circumvent or diffuse any negative energy that is headed your way. Military or political strategists are often born with this lucky symbol on their Upper Mars mounts, as are athletes and salespeople.

- **Markings on the Mars Plane:** On the plane of Mars, the most common symbol is the cross. Look carefully at your plane; since it often has so many lines moving in all kinds of directions, it might be hard to notice any particular symbol at first glance. If you do manage to spot a cross in this area of your hand, it means you are most likely very interested in studies such as alternative medicine, spirituality, or the occult.

The Mounts of the Fingers

In general, the mounts of your hands (which lie just below your fingers) represent the stores of energy that you have to dispose of regarding the particular attribute of that finger. A well-developed mount shows that you have a healthy amount of a particular quality as well as a healthy amount of interest in that area. An overdeveloped mount means that you may have too much of a particular attribute or too large a fascination with it. A flat or poorly developed mount means that you are lacking in a particular quality or that it holds little interest for you.

Actually, the mount of each finger is part of that finger, as you can see if you examine your hand closely. That is why we consider the finger mounts as a separate category from the mounts of the palm. The mount of a finger will represent the same attributes as that finger does, but will tell you where that action takes place, whereas the finger tells you of your own temperament in that area and your portrayal of that characteristic in your life.

Reading the Mounts

First, look at the size of each mount. To tell if your mount is too small or too large, compare it to the other three finger mounts on the hand. The size of your mounts will be relative, with a slender hand showing smaller mounts overall than a large, fleshy one; so, you must be willing to judge a particular mount against the others. Slightly cup your hand and then look at it sideways from the wrist upward to the fingers to see if one of the mounts dominates your hand, or if it is smaller and your hand dips down in that area. A mount that is closer to the base of the finger shows an even greater manifestation in the hand of the attributes of that finger. For instance, the higher the Jupiter mount, the more the leadership potential.

The Mount of Jupiter

The area below your forefinger, also known as the Jupiter finger, is called the mount of Jupiter. Named after the Roman god who ruled all other gods, the finger of Jupiter represents the way in which you portray yourself to the outside world and the way you are perceived in that world. It shows your sense of self-esteem and your air of authority and control, as well as your idealism, sense of honor, courage, and nerve.

A well-defined Jupiter mount indicates a strong sense of justice and optimism, as well as charisma, outgoingness, skill in managing others, and ambition. A healthy Jupiter mount in a balanced hand shows a sense of justice and willingness to help others. However, if this mount is far higher than the others, it shows a sense of ambition to rule and the desire to control and dominate others, as well as inordinate pride and self-centeredness, perhaps even bigotry. Beware of greed, a need for power, and arrogance.

If the mount is a widespread fleshy mass, but not a high one, it shows that you are an outward-directed person, are interested in society and social activity, enjoy the company of others, and expect fair play and justice for all.

If your Jupiter mount is low or weak, it means that you lack ambition, self-confidence, and a social presence. You may be strong in body, but your personality will lack forcefulness. You may also just be diverting your leadership energy into too many areas, so that none of them gets the full attention needed for successful accomplishment.

The Mount of Saturn

Your Saturn mount is located underneath your middle finger, also known as the finger of Saturn. The Saturn mount is named after the father of Jupiter, who was deposed by his son as ruler of the gods, but went on to found the golden era in Rome. Saturn is a symbol of success later in life, and his story is both a positive and a negative one.

Those with a predominant Saturn mount may be described as saturnine—gloomy and depressed. A person with too much of Saturn's influence will be too conservative, distrustful, rigid, and unwilling to bow to others. Too big a mount of Saturn means that you are too solitary, introverted, and aloof, too introspective and thoughtful. You may even become ungenerous and cynical, unable to trust anyone.

A level mount of Saturn offers a better prognosis—you are a friendly sort and think everything is for the best. You are independent enough to think for yourself, and you can balance trust and suspicion, new ideas and old values, the love of solitude and the love of friends. The person with a midsize mount of Saturn is one who exhibits just the right amount of common sense and responsibility without going overboard and becoming obsessive and moody. He is a leader in the sense of a manager or a company director, one who brings leadership qualities to an organization.

If you have too small a mount of Saturn, you lack Saturn's positive qualities: the need to look beneath the surface, the need to ponder and reflect, a sense of responsibility and organization, and the search for and love of wisdom. You may be flighty, irresponsible, disorganized, and superficial.

The Mount of Apollo

The mount of Apollo, located at the base of the ring finger, rules those attributes given to Apollo, the Roman god of the Sun who represents light and truth, poetry and art, healing and beauty. A good-sized Apollo mount means that you are outgoing and enthusiastic, talented and creative, lively and positive—a sunny and shining person. You are versatile, logical, and understanding, but your need to take the lead may sometimes make you unpopular. Your love for beauty, creativity, and self-expression may also be seen in your skills in crafts, cooking, and fashion, if not in the high arts, or at least by a deep interest in aesthetic subjects.

Too big a mount carries these things to extreme, and you become opinionated, affected, and loud, showing off your skills and possessions. You may care too much for the surface rather than the substance beneath it and become too impressed by position and fame. You may tend to overspend and burn your candle at both ends, maintaining a hedonistic lifestyle.

If your mount is too depressed, you may be dull, talentless, and insensitive to the finer things in life, willing to settle for a sterile existence; or, you may just lack energy due to illness. You hate being in the spotlight and are secretive, and you tend to cling to your in-group rather than face the outside world.

The Mount of Mercury

Mercury, the fastest of the gods, was their winged-footed messenger, and he ruled commerce and business. The mount at the base of the Mercury (small or pinky) finger controls your love for communication, expressiveness, and travel, as well as your abilities in business, teaching, and practical matters. Mercury also rules the sciences, healing arts, and even close relationships with friends and children.

A well-defined mount of Mercury shows that you are a speedy person with many interests, a good communicator, and confidant. You are versatile and flexible, and you respond well in emergencies or when action is needed. You may make a good salesperson or businessperson, public speaker, or politician. You love family life, are skilled at a number games, and are good at observation, so you can read others easily.

Too large a Mercury mount, and you talk too much, perhaps not always truthfully, and may use your gift to influence others wrongly. In any case, you will use your communications skills to

244 The Beginner's Guide to Divination

advance in life. On the other hand, a flat mount can mean you are a quiet or shy person, one who does not easily understand what is going on around you, or one who is too caught up in your life with little interest in others. It may be hard for you to communicate with a mate. You may also be impractical and confused. Many people with an underdeveloped mount of Mercury aren't successful in science or business.

The Basic Markings

Now that you understand the finger mounts and their significance, you can begin to look there for the markings that will give you further clues to the personality of the person whose hand you are reading. The following are six basic marks that can appear on the mounts of the fingers:

1. The square is a positive sign that points to a protective force.
2. The grille signifies misspent energy and lack of focus in a particular area, so that the overall attributes of the mount are too strong and too poorly directed to be effective.
3. The triangle is a sign of success that results in forward movement and gain.
4. The star shows good fortune or victory, unless it appears on the mount of Saturn, where it is a warning of problems to come.
5. The cross generally shows a negative factor or opposition in a specific area signified by that mount.
6. A dot usually represents a health concern or another negative experience.

These marks show a particular influence or quality; most finger mounts have more than one type of mark, so read the one that seems most dominant first.

CHAPTER 15

THE LINES OF THE HANDS

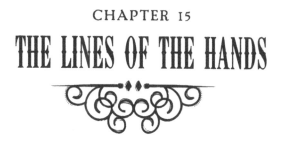

Your palm's three major lines—life line, head line, and heart line—have a lot to tell you. They can demonstrate the talents and characteristics a person is born with and how she can bring these to the forefront in everyday activities to create the kind of life she desires. No one knows exactly how these lines are formed, but we do know that they represent far more than just the bending and stretching that our hands go through every day. They are created by the body chemistry in response to what we feel, think, and experience. Here you'll learn about these three major lines as well as the line of destiny, also called your fate line, which can give you valuable information about your career, ambition, and the overall direction of your life.

The Three Major Lines

The three major lines—the life, head, and heart lines, in that order—are formed even before you are born, and they change throughout your life in response to stress and illness and according to your actions, which in turn create life changes. When you begin the portion of your reading that deals with the three major lines, you should look at them in order of importance. The first thing to look at when reading any line is the depth and width. To get an optimum reading, the line should be even in depth and width. A deep line indicates a lot of energy and interest in the subject of the line; the stronger the line, the more important it will be in indicating what the person's life is all about.

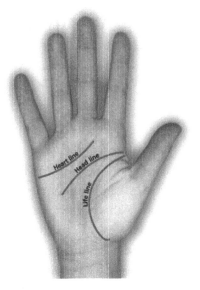

Major lines

The Life Line

The life line is the primary line of the hand, and everyone has one. As its name indicates, the life line depicts basic vitality and life force. It records physical being and warns of diseases, accidents, and other bodily events; additionally, it describes stamina, activity levels, and overall sense of liveliness.

A break or other negative mark on the line can mean any number of things, and making a prediction about the end of life can set up thoughts that lead to self-fulfilling prophecies. Think of the life line as showing you the quality—not length—of the life to come.

It's a good sign if the life lines on both hands are similar in length and shape. If the lines differ in length, you should pay more attention to the line on your dominant hand (the one that you use more often and that you write with).

Physical Condition

A long and clear line shows you have a good physical condition, good health, and the ability to overcome disease and injury. Your physical resources will be at your peak, and you'll be able to meet life's challenges with a survivor's instinct. Similarly, a life line that forks at the base of the hand shows that the owner is healthy and strong and can resist illness.

A thick life line means that you are a very physical person and perhaps a violent one; a thin life line shows a weak constitution or personality, and perhaps a very sensitive and easily injured physical body. If the line varies in thickness, you will have healthy and unhealthy periods. If the line is reddened and deeper, the life may be an energetic and intense one, but this may be seen in aggression and hostility.

Begin at the Beginning

Be very careful to assess the true beginning of the life line. If it is chained or islanded at the very start, it indicates that there is some mystery about the person's birth. Any of the other markings found at the beginning of the line would refer to the birth as well. For instance, a cross is a mark of injury or distressed birth; a square is a sign that a certain problem was overcome and the child was born healthy.

A life line that begins on the mount of Jupiter (the index finger mount) belongs to a person that seeks a lifestyle change based on ambition and the strong pursuit of his goals. If the line starts lower down at the thumb, however, the person is a homebody or resident of a small town who wants to stay there.

Between Venus and Luna Mounts

If the line arcs widely around the Venus mount, that shows a warm and receptive person who enjoys others and who loves to travel and the adventure of meeting new people. If the life line sticks close to the mount, the person is cautious, and tends to love family members and friends better than strangers and to stay at home with them; it can also indicate family commitments to aged parents. If the line actually goes into the Venus mount, the person is cold and aloof. The closer the end of the life line is to the base of the Venus mount, the more the individual wants to end life safe at home, no matter how far he has traveled. An ending at the Luna mount shows a restless nature until the end.

A longer fork that goes toward both the Luna and Venus mounts shows that person is conflicted about travel issues, wanting both security and adventure. A tassel at the end of the life line means that the end of life will see a decline of strength and perhaps a handicapping illness, which can be thwarted with proper care.

Forward-Moving Life Lines

A life line that moves up toward the Saturn (middle-finger) mount shows that the person is working very hard to succeed, but may not, after all. If the line moves toward the Apollo (ring-finger) mount, fame and fortune are to be expected.

The life line may also send up branches toward the various mounts. A line that goes up to Jupiter (index finger) shows a major advance in education or other activity that lead to achievement. A line toward Saturn shows the acquisition or property or material security. A line toward moving toward Apollo indicates success and public recognition, as well as love and affection. One branch moving toward Mercury (small finger) shows success in a commercial or artistic venture. However, if any of these lines are stopped at the heart line, there will be heartache when the venture fails, and if the line stops at the head line, the venture failed due to problems with planning or judgment.

Twin Lines

The life line can also have a twin line that gives the person life energy and added protection at times of trouble. This runs inside the life line and is called the Mars line.

But if the twin line is strong enough, the life line is considered a dual line, and it means that the person has a double existence.

He may be a twin, but he is more likely to have two diverging interests in life that are mutually exclusive.

Markings on the Life Line

These marks are standard ones that can occur on the life line. They can also be read on the head and heart lines, with some reinterpretation to account for that area of interest.

- Lines crossing the life line show worry in personal matters. Lines moving upward show progress and improvement in health matters.
- Small bars or dots across the life line show obstacles that vex us at a certain time. These keep us from advancing unless we work hard to overcome them. Bars can also be known as trauma lines and signify an emotional upheaval of some kind. A series of fine bars can mean a sensitive nature rather than actual negative events.
- A cross shows a longer lasting problem on any line, including the heart and head lines. This can mean the loss of a job, accident or other distress, and a series of these in old age can show bad health or financial ruin.
- Islands mean that there is an area of frustration, with too many directions to explore and too few resources. They are difficult periods where physical energy is low and resistance is bad, but they can be gotten through with work and attention to maintaining strength. On a life line, an island can mean a chronic disease or other debilitating physical condition.
- A chain of islands on any line shows energy being wasted, with resulting confusion and lack of focus. On the life line, they show poor health or many accidents.
- A tassel, or several lines, at the end of a line means that the energy of the line is weakened. On a life line, it means ill health or weakness.
- A fork on a line shows a decision that must be made concerning life or career as opportunities present themselves, and a

branch shows that there is a link to another area of the hand whose influence will come into play.

- A circle can mean optical problems when found on the life line, and two circles mean a more serious problem, such as blindness.
- A line dropping into the Venus mount from the life line can mean a loss such as a death in the family.

The Head Line

You have two major lines that run horizontally across your palm. The lower one, which begins at the side of the hand above the thumb and travels across the palm to end in a fork, is your head line. Just as the other two major lines, the head line appears on the palms of almost every human being—its lack is thought to indicate severe mental illness.

The head line shows our mental and intellectual life, our psychological makeup, and our intuitive abilities. It can also shed light on emotional difficulties as they influence mental health, as well as the physical condition of the head in regard to such things as headaches. The head line does not show how smart you are, but it can tell the palm reader how you think and where your skills lie. A fork on the head line can mean that a person is conflicted by too many choices.

A long head line shows intelligence, a good memory, a questioning spirit, and flexibility of interests, as well as the ability to reason and think logically. A deep and strong line means you can focus on problems and have a good ability to concentrate. A short head line shows a mental world limited to practical matters with little imaginative flair, but it can also mean that your mental strengths are focused and concentrated in one area. The stronger the head line, the more focused you are, but a weak line shows inability to concentrate and a tendency to daydream. Those of you who have a weak head line may be indecisive and unrealistic, or lack common sense.

A wavy head line points to a person who is unsteady and unable to be trusted, and a fragmented head line shows a person who is worrisome, unfocused, or with a bad memory; he may also have a tendency toward having migraines.

The Straight and Narrow

A line straight across the hand shows an analytical and logical nature. Straight head lines are seen in the hands of pragmatists who are detail-oriented and organized, who can focus well, and who are interested in the sciences and technology.

A head line that descends shows more imaginative use of the brain power. An arched head line that veers at the top toward the Jupiter mount shows that the person will be determined to succeed.

A curved line takes a more experimental and intuitive approach, and creativity is seen in career choices such as writers, linguists, and the social sciences. A very curved head line that approaches the Luna mount means the person is imaginative and idealistic, perhaps a practitioner of the creative arts such as painting and poetry. However, too deep a curve into the Luna mount can signify an interest in the subconscious area of the brain or it can mean the person lives in a world of fantasies, fear, and melancholy, unable to interact well in the real world.

From Beginning to End

A head line that begins in the Jupiter mount shows a person with great potential for success; a head line that begins inside the life line on the Mars mount can mean an ultrasensitive and hostile person who likes to cause problems and cannot follow through when it comes to getting things done.

Where the line ends is significant as well. A sloping head line that ends under the Apollo finger belongs to a person with many interests. A head line that ends below the Mercury finger likes the arts and talking about them. A forked ending shows an analytical and persuasive talker, and a fork that goes down into the Luna mount indicates the ability to make an impartial judgment.

Branching Out

It is also important to look at the lines that branch off the head line. Rising branches bring good news. If the branch rises toward Jupiter, the good news will be academic in nature. If it rises toward Saturn, the news will be career-related. If the line rises toward Apollo, expect good news related to artistic or scientific success, or personal fulfillment. Finally, business-related success is indicated by a line that branches off toward the mount of Mercury.

A rising branch at the end of an island shows an end to worry. A falling branch shows sadness and mental anguish at that point in life. And a branch to the heart line shows a person who is cold and ruled more by his head than his heart in matters of love, or an unhappy affair that changes a person's life direction.

Markings on the Head Line

Look to the section on the life line for a thorough discussion of what markings on a major line can represent. However, there is some additional information you need to know in order to interpret special marking found specifically on the head line.

- A star can mean an injury to the head.
- Small lines that criss-cross the head line can mean potential worry or headache.
- A tassel indicates a weakening in the energy of the head line, and there is confusion and possible mental illness.
- Islands on the line show worry about work or money, headaches, and the inability to concentrate, especially if found on the Saturn mount.

- A fork on a head line signifies skill in business; if it appears on the Apollo mount, it may be a writer's fork, which is said to indicate skills as a writer.

The Heart Line

The heart line appears in the upper crease of the hand, traveling up from under the Mercury finger across the hand to an area between the Jupiter and Saturn mounts. Generally, it runs above and somewhat parallel to the head line, and it is present in almost everyone.

The heart line gives an indication of a person's emotional life and emotional and physical relationships with others, as well as heart health. It shows contentment with life and feelings about affection, love, and sex, and it even indicates love for art and beauty.

In general, the shorter the heart line, the less likely the person is to be outgoing, while a longer line shows more openness and warmth overall. A heart line without branches shows a stunted emotional life.

A strong and clear heart line shows generosity and a sense of security about how others see you. A red or a darkened heart line shows that you have a temperamental approach to life, be it passionate and positive or hostile and negative, while a lighter heart line represents a colder and more distant emotional state. A faint heart line shows that you place little emphasis on emotional fulfillment.

Getting Physical

A curving heart line signifies a physical approach toward love, with sexuality an important aspect of life. A straight heart line signals a more cerebral approach to love, with more emphasis placed on fantasies and romance. Those with curved lines want to demonstrate their feelings physically and want to take the lead in physical matters. Those with a very curved heart line find sex an essential part of life. Those with a straight line need a partner who is like them in matters of the heart and mind, and they base their romantic relationships on commonalities, care, and time.

How You Might See Relationships

A high heart line that turns upward on the palm belongs to someone who sees love in an emotional and romantic way, wanting lots of reassurance and a spiritual, idealistic approach to matters of the heart. Those with lower heart lines closer to the head line are more cerebral about love, and they tend to be less demanding and more giving and supportive.

The closer the heart line ends to Saturn, the more the person sees relationships from a physical perspective. If this line is short, the physical part of the relationship is all. If such is the case with you, it's likely that you avoid emotional bonding and prefer casual flings and one-night stands instead.

On the other hand, a heart line that extends further, ending closer to Jupiter, shows an idealistic and emotional kind of love. An ending on the Jupiter mount shows a romantic soul that idealizes those it loves; when reality intrudes, these people can't handle it, and often suffer heartbreak. Endings higher up on the Jupiter finger belong to the hands of those who seek perfection in a mate. A heart line that reaches the Jupiter mount and then drops to the head line shows bad decision-making when choosing a lover.

Someone with a double heart line will be very loyal and faithful to his friends and will have added protection against any problems indicated on the main heart line.

Branches off the Heart Line

Downward branches of the heart line warn of unhappy love affairs or close friendships that end badly. If a line descends to cross the fate line, the person may lose their spouse. But branches that shoot upward signify good and positive relationships. And if your heart line has a shoot toward Mercury, you can look forward to well-earned financial success.

Often, the branches appear at the end of the heart line, where they signal diversity in terms of emotional life. Forks are common here as well. A double-forked ending shows that your life combines romance with practicality, while a triple fork indicates that your mind, heart, and energy are all in balance.

Markings on the Heart Line

Review the markings described in the section about the life line—the same interpretations will apply to markings you see on the heart line (or head line, for that matter). Additionally, here are some interpretations that are specific to the heart line:

- An island is a sign of an illegitimate or duplicitous love affair, but if it occurs below the Apollo mount, go see an eye doctor.
- A chained heart line with many islands shows a person who wants personal contact but is easily hurt and fears rejection. If you have a chained heart line, you are insecure and may fall in love too easily and too often. It can also indicate a health problem in the coronary systems and a nutritional or mineral deficiency.
- Breaks are emotional problems and warn about rejection, deceit, or unrequited love. Many breaks can means that you have the potential for repeated infidelity.
- A cross can represent potential for a coronary illness or a crisis.
- A tassel at the end of a heart line means that the energy of the line is weakened and relationships are bad or lacking.
- A circle on the heart line refers to coronary problems.

The Line of Destiny

The line of destiny has many names: most commonly the fate line, but also the Saturn line, career line, line of luck, line of achievement, or the life-task line. Generally, this line begins at the bottom of the palm and ends at the Saturn mount (the finger mount underneath your middle finger). Because Saturn is the ruler of duty, work, and security, it is indicative of the role career and responsibility will play in a person's life. Palmists look to the fate line to determine the direction of life, your control over it, and the ambition to achieve the goals you have set out for yourself. In particular, your fate line carries information about your career, ambition, material well-being, personal success, and fulfillment of goals. It is the central element of the hand and adds stability to the rest of the lines because it connects the intuitive and the practical sides of the hand. Additionally, the fate line describes public life—how people are seen by those around them.

For most people, the fate line begins at the base of the hand at the first rascette, or the bracelet line at the wrist, and it travels upward to the mount of Saturn. This is the traditional ending for the fate line, and those who have it have a secure sense of direction and purpose. A long and clear line can mean a career with the same company throughout life.

The closer to the wrist the fate line begins, the earlier a person will begin to develop a sense of responsibility and duty. His life circumstances may demand this, but it will serve a valuable purpose later on as his career develops.

The ideal fate line

A fate line that is long and strong signals an unusual sense of purpose and often belongs to those who go far in their careers. Such people have a strong sense of self and direction in life. However, a clear and consistent line running the length of the hand is rarer than you might think. Fate lines can begin and end in a surprising number of places, and all have different meanings. In general, the closer to the rascette your line of destiny begins, the better. It means that you will learn a sense of responsibility early in life.

Family Business?

If your fate line begins in the mount of Venus inside the life line, it means you had help from your family when starting off in your career, or perhaps they were too influential in making your career decision. If your fate line is joined to the life line for some distance, it shows that your career perhaps began in a family business, that they contributed to your start in life, or that you are in some other way close to and indebted to them, though not in any negative way. However, where the life line and the fate line part is where you will achieve independence from your family on your career path. However, there may be light lines of attachment between the two lines that show a strong emotional bond between you and your family.

Making Your Own Way

If your fate line begins near the life line but not within it, you will make your own way in life and determine your own priorities. Your success will rely on your ability to work and accomplish things for yourself with no outside influence.

If your fate line begins on the other side of the hand in the mount of Luna, which represents the social element, it means that your career will be in the public eye, as a politician or perhaps as an actor, but in some way that demands that you gain public approval in order to be considered a success. Your career might also be in the musical arts or in an area where you are dealing with the public (for instance, as a social worker); in any event, it will be in a field in which you are able to affect and influence others.

A Late Start

If your fate line does not begin until the middle of the hand in the plane of Mars, it may take you a long time to get started in life or to settle on a career and find your true calling. You will begin your career in struggle and uncertainty, but if your fate line reaches clearly to the Saturn mount, it will end in success based on lessons learned in the struggle.

What Happens at the End

The ending of the fate line is also of importance, for it will tell you a great deal about the eventual chance of a successful career. If the line ends beneath the Saturn finger, as is typical, security is of highest importance to you. A clean ending beneath the Saturn finger represents a good planned retirement. However, a forked or tasseled ending means a dissipation of energy and perhaps a less than positive retirement. Bars at the end of the line also mean obstacles and problems at the end of the career, and a danger of poverty and deprivation. If the fate line ends beneath the Jupiter mount, your lifework will give you high status and social standing, and you will have a brilliant career that fulfills your ambition, with power over others.

Moving Ahead

A fork or branch to the Apollo mount, or an ending of the fate line in that mount, is a sign of personal fulfillment in your career and artistic or intellectual success, usually with accompanying financial rewards. A similar fork or branch structure from the end of the fate line that ends near the Mercury mount means success in business or the sciences, or perhaps a special talent for persuasion and conversation.

Getting Off Track

However, a fate line that ends at the head line shows that your career is hampered by errors of judgment and intellectual missteps. And if your fate line ends short in a dead end at the heart line, your career may be sidetracked either by an emotional disruption, such as an affair at work, or perhaps by a heart condition.

If the heart line is deep and cuts through the fate line, interrupting it, it means that an emotional attachment has caused a financial fallback—this is often the sign of the death of a marriage partner that leaves the widow with too little income, or a deceased business partner without the insurance that will keep the company solvent. But if your heart line merges equally and gently with your fate line, you will have it all—love and affection, wealth, power, honor, and fame.

Markings on the Fate Line

Like the other lines, the markings on the fate line let us know more about what we have in store for us. Classic markings can take on new meanings when applied to the line of destiny. For example, a break in the line of destiny shows a change in job or career, and a sudden break is an unexpected change; an overlapping break means a change you controlled, so it might not have a negative outcome as an unexpected change would have. Many breaks signal many changes and the inability to take off in one direction in a career. A fate line that has many breaks, islands, and stops shows that a person has many changes of career or a series of unproductive jobs.

A short and light bar on the line is an obstacle that is short-term and may be gotten around with effort, such as a problem supervisor. If the bar is heavier than the fate line itself, it means a problem that is very disturbing to the owner of the hand. A series of bars can mean insurmountable obstacles.

A fork can suggest a change in career, or at the very least exploration of a new career path. Grille patterns with lines in both vertical and horizontal patterns can point to burdensome worries.

An island on the fate line shows trouble and frustration, dissatisfaction, or financial shortfalls. At the beginning of the fate line, an island can signify a mysterious origin, just as it can on the life line. This used to be thought of as a mark of illegitimacy or adoption, but now it is seen as a sign of some unknown influence at the beginning of life.

A cross on the fate line, if seen at the beginning of the line, can show the loss of a parent early in life. A cross farther along on the line means a crisis or a change in the person's life, and this crisis will have a lasting effect on that life. A cross that appears next to the fate line may represent a crisis or change, but it can also be significant of something that will effect a positive change in the person's life by calling on untapped talents. It may cause a re-examination of old beliefs and a switch to new and more effective habits.

A square on the fate line shows that you are protected from a problem. It can be a warning if it occurs in midlife to give the hand's owner a chance to prepare for problems, and it can also allow the owner of the hand to take a risk, knowing that he is somewhat protected.

A triangle between the fate and the life line signifies victory in military endeavors or at least winning a major battle if the owner of the hand is a civilian.

A star on the line of destiny is a sudden shock or disturbance in the career, a sudden rise in the energy field that causes a negative situation. If it happens early on the line, this could mean a familial emergency, such as a move or loss of fortune, that took place without warning but left emotional scars.

CHAPTER 16

PALMISTRY AND THE DIVINATION OF LOVE

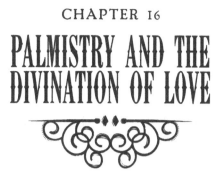

Looking for the perfect mate? Let palmistry be your guide, and you will need to look no further than the lines, mounts, and marking on your hands—and the ones on the hands of your potential partner. You can keep your fingers crossed while you tempt fate, but you can't escape the destiny of true love. Don't miss the signs that say, "All systems go!"

What is the first thing you do when you are introduced to a person? In many cases, you shake hands with each other. Thus, the first impression you form about the new acquaintance is made, at least in part, by the type of handshake you receive—its warmth, firmness, and length.

Since hands are generally out in the open and are easy to see, you can get an impression about the person you are meeting by simply looking at his or her hand. The shape of the hand can show you the level of passion and feeling in a person, his or her ability to commit, and other important personality traits. It is also possible to see what compatibility there will be between two people by looking at their hands.

Lovers often begin by holding hands, and much can be learned from the warmth of that hand, its stiffness or pliability, and its softness or hardness. Hands are just basically sensual, the organs by which we feel, the way in which we reach out to others, and we can learn a lot about sensuality from them.

The Shape of Things to Come

Remember the four hand shapes introduced in Chapter 13? Well, you can tell a lot just by noting which hand shape your new acquaintance has. Here is a rundown of the interpretations of what hands say about a person. At most, you will get a good idea about the person whose hand you are holding, and at the very least you can meet a lot of new people by offering to hold hands with them.

- **Conical hands:** These are "Air" hands; they signal a person who enjoys having lots of friends but who is very choosy when looking for a partner. This person adheres to a moral code and likes routines.
- **Pointed hands:** These are "Water" hands; they represent people who bring their naiveté into relationships, sometimes being taken advantage of by those who are not as idealistic as they are. Those with Water hands are highly romantic, sensitive to beauty, fond of gifts, attracted to sensuality, and bored by the routine.
- **Spatulate hands:** These are "Fire" hands; they usually belong to people who have widespread emotional ups and downs—frequently, their close and caring friends are called upon to support them in crisis after crisis as they change partners. They like variety, excitement, and new experiences in all areas of life, including the bedroom, and they are very physical people.
- **Square hands:** These are "Earth" hands. They point to honesty, sincerity, dependability, and support. While those with Earth hands may not be the demonstrative types, you can always count on them. Their hands are crafty and have the kind of creativity needed to make a home.

Looking deeply into your individual potential for marital happiness, if you have a well-padded hand, you tend to be warm, passionate, and energetic. You are emotionally healthy and enjoy earthly pleasures, including food and drink. If you have a thinner hand, you are less passionate about life, cooler and more withdrawn. Harder hands belong to those who are less flexible and more demanding of others, while softer hands reveal a lower libido and a passive nature that waits to be given to rather than reaching out to give.

Major Lines for Love

Once you've looked at the basic shape and feel of the hand, it is time to move on to the lines on the palm. Since love and relationships are such a vital part of life, many of them come into play when you are looking for answers in this area. It is the overall pattern of the lines rather than each specific line that will give you the information you are looking for. For clues, look specifically at the heart, life, and fate lines, as well as the markings around them.

The Heart Line

The heart line is a good place to start when looking at your palm to see what your relationships will be like. This line describes both feelings and libido, and shows how well a person manages to bond emotionally with others. If your heart line is long, deep, and without blemishes, you are a devoted friend, secure in relationships, and have an affectionate and loyal nature. Here are the features that you should look for when reading the heart line for love potential:

- **Chains and islands:** Your feelings are changeable and short-lived. You want intimacy but fear commitment, so you waver and are insecure. Other people may see you as cold and unapproachable.
- **Shape of the line:** If you have a straight heart line, you are very cool and rational, attuned to the mental image of what you want and willing to wait for it. Generally, you are the type

of person who makes decisions based on what makes sense. If you have a curved heart line, you are more emotional, moved by your thoughts and desires, and willing to move more physically and aggressively toward goals.

- **Space between head and heart line:** If the space is wide, you are tolerant and willing to live and let live. If the space is narrow, you are secretive and ill at ease in many social situations because you find it hard to say how you feel.

Also check where your heart line ends. If it tapers off under Saturn, you are a very physical person but one who is controlled by the rationality of Saturn rather than by sheer romance. If your heart line ends under Jupiter, your love life will have a strong component of an idealized view of your partner. You are loyal, but this may veer over into possessiveness. (If you have a curved heart line that ends here, it shows that your love affair may be with all of humanity rather than one person.)

The Head Line

The head line may not be as important an area in terms of providing direct information about your romantic relationships as the heart line, but it will give you valuable clues about your love life as it fits into your overall life.

First, compare the head and heart lines. If the head line is heavier than the heart line, you will look for a partner who can be a good companion and who gives you mental stimulation. You will think before you act on sexual feelings. If the heart line is heavier than the head line, it is just the opposite. You will be ruled more by feelings and your need for passion.

If your head line is straight across the palm, you are practical and realistic about love and you have a less romantic view of things. You also tend to be more traditional about the social mores. If your head line drops downward to the mount of

Luna, you are more romantic about love, and the bigger the dip downward, the more imagination and illusion play a role in your hopes and dreams.

The Life Line

Because it lies so near to the mount of Venus, the life line can provide many hints about a person's love life. The life line represents health, so a strong one shows you have much passion to give, while a weak one points to a limitation in the amount of energy you have to give to your physical nature.

If you have a life line that makes a wide sweep across the palm, leaving room for a large mount of Venus, you have a great deal of love to give and energy to put to use in the sexual arena. You are likely an extrovert and outwardly directed. On the other hand, a life line close to the thumb constricts the mount of Venus and shows a lower sex drive.

Branches that shoot off from the inside of the life line toward the mount of Venus portray important relationships, either with lovers, close friends, or children; check the time on the life line to see when these relationships may develop. If they continue to follow the line, the relationship will remain strong; if they diverge and head to the thumb, things will get difficult.

The Line of Destiny

While the lines that emerge from the life line are valuable indicators of relationships, you should also look at how the fate line and the life line are related. A fate line that touches the life line or even begins inside it shows a strong influence of your parents in your selection of a mate. You will want a partner that will help replace the parent of the opposite sex: a fatherlike caretaker if you are a woman and a nurturing caregiver if you are a man. On the contrary, if the fate line begins far from the life line in the middle of the palm, you will be far more independent in selecting your mate. And if it begins at the mount of Luna, your relationship will be one in which you look for a godlike and demanding figure to worship.

The Venus Mount

Turning away from the lines of the hand, we'll look at one of the most important elements in our sexual and romantic life. The mount of Venus, as you might guess, is where the sexual force lives in the hand—and the higher it is, the sexier you are. It represents not only the generative process but also your capacity to make and keep good friends.

Check the size of the mount of Venus. If it takes up more than a third of your palm, you have a lot of physical passion; if it's smaller than that, you don't really express your passions in a physical way. If the life line goes through your mount of Venus, you do not hold sex as an important element in your life. This is also true if your mount of Venus is flat or small.

The Girdle of Venus

Find your heart line and look above it for a circular line between the bases of the Jupiter and Mercury fingers. If you have one, it is called the girdle of Venus and is an indicator of a very sexual or emotional nature. This is particularly true if it is accompanied by a mount of Venus that is large and strong.

A shorter girdle of Venus is a sign of emotional responsiveness, and it can be found in those in the performing arts who are both sensitive to beauty and who can share it with others. If the line is clear, you can balance your strong emotional responses in a healthy way and not be overwhelmed by them. On the other hand, a long and unclear girdle of Venus with many breaks shows you will have trouble with finding a good outlet for your emotional responsiveness. You may make unwise decisions or act out in extremely unproductive ways.

Happily Ever After?

If your hand shows that the sexual side of life is not the strongest of your urges, you need not despair. Happiness in relationships is found not so much in the sexual side of things but in compatibility. Good relationships are based on having things in common, and these can be found in many areas: intellectual pursuits, sports, the arts, travel, and the outdoors.

The key is finding a partner with mutual interests and a nature similar to yours. Two people with lower sexual interest will be happier than if someone with a high sexual interest marries someone with a lower interest in the physical aspects of life. Then, too, opposites do attract in certain ways. Someone with a more dominant sexual need might do well to find someone who likes to take a submissive role.

Compatible Elements

The first place to look for compatibility—be it with a partner, family member, or friend—is in the shape of the hand. It goes without saying that two people with the same hand types will be compatible:

- Two Air-handed people can master their emotions and will be on the same mental plane, sharing ideas and activities.
- Two Earth-handed people will get along because they work hard to build a solid relationship.
- Two Water-handed people will live as soul mates, but their inattention to practical matters may get them into trouble.

- Two Fire-handed people may have more of a problem than the other three groups, unless their dips and peaks complement each other's. They must take turns being high and low, seeking and getting attention.

You should compare also your life, heart, and head lines with those of your partner to see how compatible you are—and how to make the most of what you have and overcome differences.

First, look at your heart lines to see how similar they are. If they are the same length and move in the same direction, you understand each other well and have much in common. However, if one of you has a curved heart line, indicative of warmth and spirit, and the other a straight one, showing cooler emotions, this could mean trouble—or a chance to balance each other and work together to create a strong relationship that takes both the rational and emotional into account.

The same is true of the head line. If you have a curved head line and your partner has a straight one, you will differ on issues of practicality and romance. This is an indication that you should bring both of these things into your lives, strengthening your relationship by making it more multifaceted.

Differences in the life line show differing health and energy levels as well as differences between introverts and extroverts, which can be overcome. But if the life lines and mounts of Venus show differences in sexual appetite, these are hard areas in which to find compromises.

Overall, the differences in a relationship must be taken into account. Stresses and arguments that arise from them can cause trouble, or we can use them as ways to learn acceptance and tolerance of differences. At best, these challenges can force us to grow and to learn another person's point of view and expand our own, overcoming our own limitations of thought and behavior. If the devotion is there, it may be worth it.

INDEX